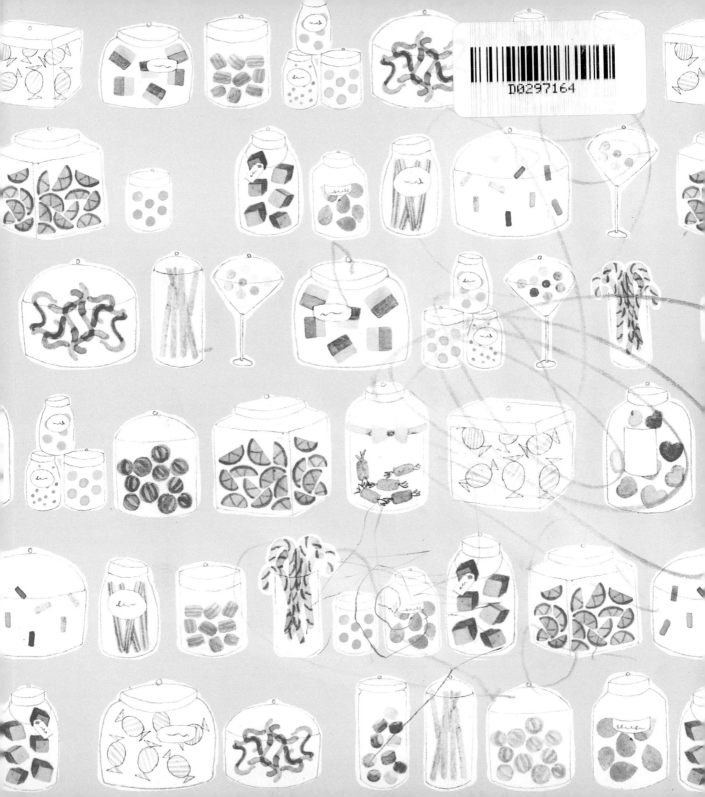

Aberdeenshire

COUNCIL

Aberdeenshire Libraries
www.aberdeenshire.gov.uk/libraries
Renewals Hotline 01224 661511

For my parents, John and Sandra, with love.

MRS BEETON'S

HOMEMADE SWEETSHOP

Our favourite sweets to make, give and enjoy

ISABELLA BEETON & GERARD BAKER

W&N
WEIDENFELD & NICOLSON

CONTENTS

—

INTRODUCTION

When Isabella Beeton first published her *Book of Household Management* in 1861, confectionery would have been a rare and expensive treat for all but the wealthiest members of Victorian society.

Whereas today we are used to buying sweets from almost every shop and supermarket, for the newly married Mrs Beeton, confectionery was mainly sold in high-class bakers as well as confectioners, as the two trades developed hand in hand over the centuries.

Before her marriage to Sam Beeton, Isabella certainly had shown an interest in sweet making (as well as baking), as she undertook training with the young confectioner William Barnard in the High Street at Epsom. Barnard belonged to a family of shop- and innkeepers and it is perhaps no surprise to us today that Isabella's family was suspicious of her practical interest as they wanted only the best for their eldest daughter. Isabella had developed a love of pastry making and confectionery while at finishing school in southern Germany, and so her parents indulged the young Isabella in her very modern interest as this was the only sort of culinary training that was thought suitable for young women to undertake.

For the general population, sweets were a treat to look forward to at festive gatherings such as Christmas or Easter. Throughout the country, annual agricultural fairs were made more special by the presence of journeyman sweet makers who travelled from county to county, selling their delights. Candy canes, barley sugar, perhaps even a block of the newly developed Fry's chocolate would have vied with the best luxuries money could buy. As Isabella grew up, it is very possible that she would have marvelled at sweets on sale at her father's Epsom racecourse grandstand as the crowds enjoyed their day at the races.

Virtually all sweets are based on sugar, which was historically prized, partly because of its rarity and therefore its expense. Since the earliest 14th and 15th-century written recipes, honey had been used to sweeten fruit, bread and nut pastes to create some of the earliest British confections. Sugar was reserved for creating magical sculptures and for crystallising fruits and flowers, something that Elizabeth I was particularly fond of.

Medieval confectioners and medics considered sugar to be the most perfectly balanced food, and as such afforded it medicinal qualities as it was thought to be able to bring the body back to perfect health. Boiled sugar sweets, strongly flavoured with menthol, aniseed or liquorice (which we still enjoy today) give a hint that sugar has for centuries been considered beneficial to health.

As the worldwide production of sugar grew in the 16th and 17th centuries its use percolated down from the royal court to be used much more widely in baking and confectionery, so that when Isabella was writing her book, it was more affordable and relatively widely available to the home cook.

Making sweets in Isabella's day, however, was intensive labour, often requiring great patience and dedication. White sugar came in the form of huge cones, or loaves, of hard crystalline sugar that had to be crushed and powdered to use in preserves or to candy fruit. To make even the simplest barley sugar twist, hardworking housewives had to remove the impurities in the sugar with egg whites.

Around the time that Isabella was writing her *Book of Household Management*, pioneering chocolatiers like Francis Fry were developing the very first chocolate bars, which Isabella considered special enough to be presented with a range of fruits and nuts at the end of a dinner. Meanwhile, in Switzerland, Rudolphe Lindt and Daniel Peter were taking advantage of Nestlé's powdered milk to add creaminess to the very first milk chocolate.

The Victorian sweetshop would have contained many of the sweets we still eat today – barley sugars, nougat and chocolate bars to name a few. Walk into an 'old-fashioned' sweetshop today and you will almost without doubt be transported back to your childhood. Jars of Everton toffee, sherbet fountains, fruit jellies and mint fondants abound and so many of them are derived from historic recipes. Since Isabella wrote her book, technology has allowed confectioners to appeal to our love of sugar in ever more imaginative ways – but we never forget that simple 'hit' that our first taste of confectionery gave us.

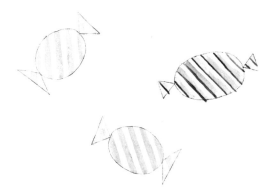

THE RECIPES

Isabella Beeton published many recipes for traditional confections, notably fruit pastes and jellies, which in Victorian England were a means of preserving fruits and nuts with sugar in order to prolong their shelf life in the kitchen. Isabella's recipes escort the reader through the seasons – from making candied orange slices in the winter, through to summer preserves of raspberry and strawberry, and finally autumnal apple pastes, similar to the Spiced Apple and Cinnamon Pastilles recipes in this book.

Since Isabella's time of writing, much has changed in the sweetshop – the development of fudge, soft caramels, and the ever expanding range of chocolate available for the home cook to use. This book reflects the evolution of our traditional sweetshop and is packed full of new recipes for you to try at home.

If you have never made sweets before, there are so many simple recipes here that are achievable for the novice cook. Fruit pastes and fresh fruit jellies are delicious and a great place to begin as they require only basic techniques. For the more adventurous, there are tempting recipes for moulded chocolates, nougats and fudges. All the recipes have been devised to work in a simple modern kitchen with little special equipment – so go ahead and experiment. You can be sure that whatever the end result looks like, your friends and family will be glad to help you sample them.

Sweets, in all their variety, have an enduring appeal to young and old alike – and what nicer gift to give than a pretty box of homemade caramels or fudge? Why not enter Mrs Beeton's sweetshop and see what you can create?

WHAT IS SUGAR?

Granulated white sugar is derived from two main sources: sugar cane and sugar beet. Until the mid-18th century, sugar cane was the only known source of what we know as sugar, be it brown or white. Other natural sweeteners existed of course, but these – honey, and tree syrups such as maple and birch – are less suitable for sugar work. Only pure sugar, consisting of sucrose crystals, was capable of being melted and then worked into magical clear sheets, moulded into fantastical shapes and spun into webs.

Papua New Guinea is thought to have been the original home to sugar cane plants that, although now extinct in the wild, are cultivated in warmer latitudes as far apart as Mauritius and Jamaica. It is thought that the Persians first perfected the art of refining crystalline white sugar around the 7th century AD, transporting it in large cones ('sugar loaves') to the royal kitchens of Europe.

Most of the sugar we use today is still derived from the stems of the giant sugar cane plant, while a smaller portion is produced from the root of the sugar beet – a relative of the white form of beetroot.

Sugar from sugar beets was first manufactured commercially in early 19th century France when the blockade of Napoleonic France resulted in a rush to find an alternative source to cane sugar. Beet is still used for sugar production, and although it is only ever used to make white sugar, has the advantage of being able to be grown in temperate, as opposed to tropical, climates.

In chemical terms, granulated white sugar is virtually pure sucrose, one of many different sugars that exist in nature. It is made up from one molecule of glucose (also known as dextrose) and one of fructose. These two small molecules have the same chemical formula; they are just different shapes and have quite different properties and flavours, fructose being much sweeter. When sugar is heated and dissolved in liquid, the sucrose molecules break into these two simpler sugars.

The confectioner needs to control the way that these two sugars, glucose and fructose, melt and recombine so that the consistency of the end product can be carefully regulated.

Grainy tablet, silky smooth fudge and glassy boiled sweets all have different textures that result from the way the confectioner controls the sugar melting and recrystallisation process.

WORKING WITH SUGAR

Although early confectioners understood some aspects of the behaviour of sugar, it was only with the development of the thermometer that they were able to codify exactly what happens to a solution of sugar heated to particular temperatures.

As a syrup is heated, and then boiled, water is driven off and the concentration of sugar in the syrup increases. At relatively low temperatures – around 113–116°C, when there is still a lot of water in the syrup, the syrup will form soft strands when dropped into cold water – the syrup will be thick and jelly-like when cold. At higher temperatures, the syrup will be more firm when cold, up to the point when it will form hard glass-like balls – at around 145–150°C. When the sugar starts to brown and form caramel, the sugar will be brittle and glass-like and easily burn as there is no more water left in the syrup.

Before the widespread use of the thermometer, cooks devised descriptions of the consistencies of syrups when boiled to different temperatures, such as 'thread', 'soft ball' and 'hard crack' – this is the method Isabella would have had to follow. Typically, a range of temperatures was given for each sugar stage – this is simply because early thermometers were not as precise as they are today. While these ranges can be useful if you do not have an accurate temperature probe or thermometer, in the recipes in this book I will refer only to exact temperatures. The chart overleaf shows the main ones that you will encounter.

Crystallisation control

Although sucrose is capable of being dissolved in liquids, it is also capable of recrystallising if the solution is strong enough or saturated (meaning that you can't dissolve any more sugar into it). The temperature at which this recrystallisation takes place determines the speed at which this happens, and also to some extent the size of crystals that form.

Some sweets, such as caramels, have a very smooth texture that can be ruined if the mixture has crystallised; whereas in fondant or fudge making, crystallisation is carefully monitored to ensure that only fine, delicate crystals form. At other times, sweet mixtures are stirred while still very hot which makes large crystals form quickly – in the case of crystalline candies. When making sheer caramels, or brittle spun sugar, it is important not to allow, or accidentally encourage, crystals of sugar or, more accurately, sucrose, to form.

A major consideration for the confectioner, then, is the control of this process, and factors such as the presence of other crystals – which is why a wet pastry brush is used to brush down the insides of the pan during cooking, and why we beat fudges at different temperatures to agitate the syrup.

SUGAR STAGES

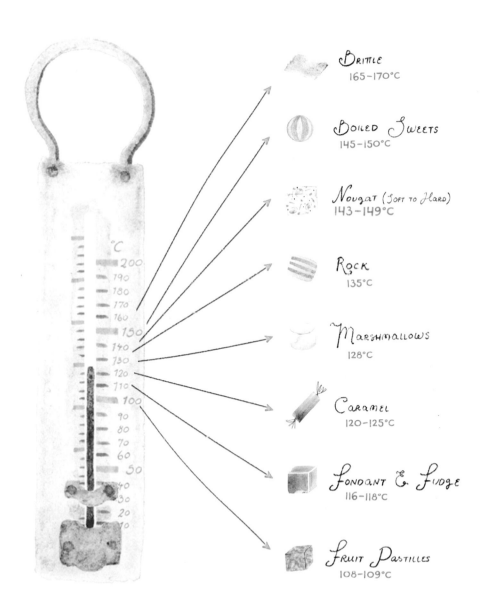

Brittle
165-170°C

Boiled Sweets
145-150°C

Nougat (Soft to Hard)
143-149°C

Rock
135°C

Marshmallows
128°C

Caramel
120-125°C

Fondant & Fudge
116-118°C

Fruit Pastilles
108-109°C

INGREDIENTS

Isabella would be amazed at the sheer variety of sugar, chocolate and other sweet-making ingredients available to us in the 21st century. Most large supermarkets and specialist baking shops now sell many of the items listed below but the online suppliers on page 202 are also good resources.

SUGAR PRODUCTS

Granulated

Virtually pure sucrose, white granulated sugar is suitable for all sweets. It is widely available, and an essential storecupboard ingredient.

Caster

Finer than granulated, and more expensive, caster sugar dissolves more quickly but is otherwise identical to granulated. It is useful for giving fruit pastilles a fine coating.

Icing sugar

This is simply very finely ground, granulated sugar with a little added desiccant to keep it dry. It is used for decorating sweets, or dusting boiled sweets to prevent them sticking together.

Demerara

A light brown sugar with large hard crystals. Originally made in Demerara, Guyana, this sugar contains a small amount of residual molasses. Very useful when a light toffee flavour is required, such as when making caramels.

Muscovado

A soft sticky sugar that contains a large quantity of residual molasses. It is a particularly flavourful sugar that is often used in toffee and fudge making. Dark muscovado is sometimes known as Barbados sugar; a light version is also available. The darker the sugar, the higher the molasses content.

Soft light and brown sugars

These are interchangeable with muscovado in most recipes. Darker sugars will more easily overcook and burn at high temperatures so are best used for fudge whereas the lighter varieties are more useful when making high-temperature toffees.

Molasses

Black and sticky, molasses is essentially what remains of the cane sugar juice after sugar is refined. Molasses lends a strong flavour to toffees and caramel but it can dominate, so use cautiously.

Golden syrup

Golden syrup is made from white sugar that is heated with an acid to create a mixture that rarely crystallises. A lightly flavoured syrup that is often used in the same way that liquid glucose is.

Liquid glucose

This viscous clear syrup is used not as a sweetener, but to interrupt the formation of sucrose crystals when boiling syrups. It is widely available in small tubes from most supermarkets. Useful for making all boiled sweets and caramels.

OTHER SOURCES OF SWEETNESS

Jaggery

An unrefined sugar that is extracted from the sugar palm. Made in south-east Asia, it has a distinct acid note and is delicious in caramels.

Honey

Produced by bees from nectar, honey comes in a wide variety of flavours. Bees secrete an enzyme that splits sucrose into glucose and fructose, which makes honey both taste particularly sweet and which also causes it to burn more quickly than a sucrose syrup. Sweets containing honey therefore are usually cooked to a lower temperature than those made purely from sugar/sucrose. Nougat is frequently made with a portion of honey.

Maple syrup

The boiled sap of maple and other trees can be reduced to make a thick syrup. Prior to the introduction of honeybees to the New World, maple syrup was the only source of sugar to the population of North America. As 50 gallons of sap are needed to produce a single cup of syrup, it is rarely made domestically.

Corn syrup

Derived from maize, corn syrup can contain both glucose and fructose, and in sweet production is used to disrupt crystallisation in much the same way as liquid glucose. It is more commonly used in America than in the UK. You can substitute half the quantity of glucose syrup for corn syrup in any recipe.

Fructose

Fructose is sometimes used to replace sucrose in so-called low sugar diets. It is particularly sweet and is rarely used as a seperate ingredient in the domestic kitchen as its health benefits are questionable. Fructose is available in powdered form from health food shops and many supermarkets.

CHOCOLATE AND COUVERTURE

Chocolate that is designed for use by professional chocolatiers usually has a greater proportion of cocoa butter to cocoa, which makes it more fluid, and therefore easier to use when melted. This is known as couverture.

Cocoa mass is the name given to the cocoa and cocoa butter mixture that forms the basis of dark and milk chocolates. Different proportions of these two determine how fluid the chocolate will be when melted.

Dark chocolate

This should contain only cocoa mass and sugar and perhaps a little flavouring such as vanilla. The percentage of cocoa mass is usually indicated on the package and legally must be over 39%. Typically, chocolatiers use cooks chocolate known as couverture with between 60–80% cocoa mass.

Milk chocolate

Concentrated milk is added to cocoa mass to make milk chocolate, which also contains sugar and often flavouring such as vanilla. Milk chocolate typically is softer than dark, and requires delicate handling when used to make moulded chocolates. Milk chocolate melts at a slightly lower temperature than dark chocolate, so ensure that you always heat it carefully.

White chocolate

Milk is also used in the manufacture of white chocolate, which contains no cocoa solids at all, just cocoa butter, and is usually flavoured with vanilla because cocoa butter has no real flavour of its own. White chocolate is the softest and melts at a lower temperature than its darker cousins. As such it requires particularly careful heating and handling at all times.

Cook's chocolate

If you want to make fine chocolates such as those shaped in moulds, it is best to use a high-quality cook's chocolate which is made to be more liquid when melted than the type of chocolate bar you would buy for eating. Avoid cheap cook's chocolate, especially the types that have vegetable oil or fat added, as these are inferior both in flavour and texture. Suppliers are listed at the back of the book which offer good mail order prices.

OTHER USEFUL INGREDIENTS

Butter

Most of the recipes in this book that use fat specify unsalted butter for preference because it has the finest flavour. As it does not keep for as long as salted butter, only buy what you will use within a week and store any excess in the freezer well wrapped. If you only have salted butter to hand, though, it is a perfectly acceptable alternative.

Oil

A flavourless oil is sometimes used to line tins or to stop your knife sticking to toffees and other sweets when cutting them up. Almond oil is the best for this because it is so light and is available from continental food markets and delicatessens. Sunflower oil is the safest oil to use if you are making sweets to sell or give away as it is less allergenic than nut oils.

Cream of tartar

This is one of the components of baking powder and is an acid ingredient that we use when making syrups as it inhibits the tendency of crystals to form, which would otherwise spoil the texture of your confection.

Citric acid

A sour tasting powder that is used in place of lemon juice in food manufacture and which is very useful when making fruit sweets. A small pinch can be used to sharpen the flavour of boiled fruit sweets or pastilles. It is not suitable for use in dairy-based confections, however, as it will cause milk and cream to curdle.

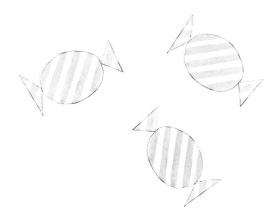

Gelatine

This can be bought in either powdered or leaf form, and I recommend the latter as it has little if any flavour.

Pectin powder

A gelling agent that is used in jams and jellies, pectin powder is used to make the fruit pastille recipes in this book. It can be bought in small quantities and keeps well stored in an airtight container. Liquid pectin tends to be more widely available but, sadly, does not give consistent results.

Colourings

We use colours to add interest to our boiled sweets and occasionally to fruit jellies and fondants. The best kind to use are paste colours, which are very concentrated and will not dilute the recipe, unlike liquid colours. It is sensible, then, to use a cocktail stick or the tip of a knife to add these colours in tiny quantities. Paste colours are widely available from supermarkets and specialist cake decorating shops.

Flavourings

For flavouring your sweets, search out the best natural extracts, as opposed to artificial flavourings. Online and high street kitchen shops are a great resource for these.

Decorations

Many supermarkets and specialist baking shops sell a fabulous range of sprinkles, nut nibs, gold leaf and other decorations that can be used for your confections. Try to resist the temptation to buy too many at once, and store in a dark cool place as colours quickly fade if exposed to the light.

EQUIPMENT

You will no doubt already have most of the equipment you need for making simple sweets, but here is a comprehensive list of kit that will make life easier in the kitchen. Suppliers of more specialised items can be found on page 202.

TEMPERATURE PROBES AND THERMOMETERS

There are many different sugar thermometers and temperature probes on the market. A traditional sugar thermometer is just as good as a digital probe: both are only good, however, if they read accurately. Regularly test your probe or thermometer: the easiest way to do this is to place it in a small pan of water and bring to the boil; it should read 100°C. If the thermometer or probe does not read accurately, it may be time to replace the thermometer, or replace the battery in the probe.

For sugar work, I recommend a digital probe with a metal cable (that won't melt) which can be clipped onto the side of the pan as your confection cooks.
This is useful as it prevents the probe slipping into the base of the pan, which is very messy. A probe with an alert system is really useful as you can allow a syrup to simmer away on its own and set the alarm to sound when the syrup approaches the desired temperature.

When you are testing the temperature of a boiling liquid, try to keep the tip of the probe mid-way in the liquid – if it touches the base of the pan it will give you an inaccurate reading. If you are using a sugar thermometer, preheat it in warm water before using to prevent the glass cracking.

If you plan on doing a lot of chocolate work, a spatula probe is a great investment. The thermometer is in the spoon itself so takes a direct reading of the temperature of the chocolate, which can change very quickly. Just make sure that the probe is thoroughly dry before using, otherwise your chocolate will seize. An alternative would be to use a normal probe as above, but try to find a responsive one that has a digital read-out as chocolate is very sensitive to small changes in temperature.

MIXERS AND BLENDERS

A free-standing food mixer is brilliant for any recipes that involve beaten egg whites such as nougat and marshmallows, as a handheld electric whisk is not powerful enough to beat the mixture. A food processor is useful, especially for chopping fruits and nuts, and a small hand blender is essential for making fruit juices and for emulsifying ganache fillings for chocolates.

OTHER USEFUL EQUIPMENT

Pans

For making toffees, boiled sweets, caramels and fudge, you'll need a pan large enough to contain the mixture as it boils and bubbles up, but also, importantly, one that will give you enough depth of liquid for you to easily measure the temperature with a sugar thermometer. I use a heavy bottomed stainless-steel pan in two sizes: 16–20cm (2–3-litre) and 20–30cm (3–4-litre).

Baking trays and tins

Use solid, non-stick tins and line them with non-stick baking paper where the recipe suggests. A couple of large baking trays are essential, along with a smaller baking tray for setting fudges and so on, and a couple of deeper, square tins are also useful.

Digital scales

When making confectionery, accurate measurements are essential, so digital scales are preferable. You can set your pan or mixing bowl straight onto the scales and re-set them to zero after adding each ingredient, saving on washing up.

Measuring spoons

For accuracy, always use measuring spoons as opposed to your kitchen cutlery and unless otherwise specified, use level spoonfuls for the recipes in this book.

Marble slab or granite surface

This is useful for tempering chocolate (see page 150) and for pulling boiled sweets such as acid drops as it will cool the syrup quickly. An alternative is a silicone mat set in a large baking tray. Many kitchen counters will warp if you pour a hot syrup directly onto them, so be very careful always to use a heatproof mat underneath your baking tray if you do not have a stone surface of some sort.

Silicone non-stick baking mat

These heatproof non-stick mats are great for tempering work, for cooling syrups when making pulled toffees and for general use in the kitchen whenever you need a reliable non-stick liner. It is worth investing in a couple of sizes, but one large enough to line your biggest baking tray will be most useful for the recipes in this book. I prefer Silpat mats as they are virtually indestructible and will last a long time. Other brands are available, but I find them too thin.

Heatproof silicone spatula

A silicone spatula is ideal for stirring syrups as it won't warp and will not hold flavours, unlike a wooden spoon. But if you don't have one, a clean wooden spoon can be used instead.

Palette knife

An indispensable tool for lifting, spreading and smoothing. A palette knife with an offset blade is particularly useful because it gives you a little more control and leverage.

Metal scraper

With its wide, metal blade and wooden handle this is useful for turning cooling syrups when making boiled sweets and is similarly used when tempering chocolate. It's also handy for cutting boiled sweets and toffees.

Pastry brush

This is used for brushing down the insides of the pan when cooking sugar syrups. Choose a natural haired brush as the bristles will not melt in hot syrups. Make sure that you are scrupulous in cleaning your brush in hot soapy water, and dry it thoroughly before storing.

Paintbrush

For applying colours and gold leaf, a sable-haired brush is the best and these are available from craft shops.

Vinyl gloves

These disposable gloves should be used to protect your skin when cooking syrups. I also recommend wearing them when handling melted chocolate for truffle making, and also for handling finished sweets so that you don't fingerprint them.

Muslin

For straining fruit juices and syrups, muslin squares or rolls are available from kitchenware shops. These can be reused, but make sure that you do not wash them in strongly scented washing powder or your jelly will be tainted.

Disposable piping bags

Handy for piping ganache when making truffles.

Melon baller

Perfect for forming praline centres and firmer ganaches. If you don't have one, a teaspoon will do.

Dipping forks

These make the task of enrobing truffles in melted chocolate much easier. A small fork with fine tines can be used in its place.

Polycarbonate moulds

These are used for making filled chocolates and are much better than the silicone ones as they are sturdier and can be cleaned much more easily.

NOTE ON HOBS

The recipes in this book were tested on both electric and gas hobs. The two perform slightly differently, and induction will perform differently again, so you should read the advice below before starting to cook.

Electric hobs – these are the best for cooking syrups because they heat the base of the pan evenly more often than not. You should begin cooking the syrup over a low heat until the sugar has fully dissolved before boiling the syrup to its finished temperature.

Gas hobs – gas flames can be more challenging to use when making syrups, especially if you are using a small pan. This is because the flames can lick around the sides of the pan and caramelise the syrup before the base of the pan reaches the required temperature. If you are using a gas hob, you should begin to cook your syrup over a small flame that directly heats just the base of the pan on a low heat, before transferring the pan to a higher heat or a larger flame.

Induction hobs – these can easily be used to make syrups, but you should remember that the heat comes from the base of the pan, and not from the hob itself. This is particularly relevant when you are cooking syrups to a high temperature as you cannot arrest the cooking (see page 28) by dipping the base of the pan into cold water. Instead, you should have a clean pan to hand into which you can quickly pour the finished syrup before it overcooks, otherwise it will continue to cook and may burn.

STORING SWEETS

Because sugar absorbs moisture from the atmosphere, it is advisable to store all sweets in an airtight tin or container, preferably out of the sun in a cool room (don't store in the fridge unless otherwise specified). Even those sweets that are pure sugar will eventually spoil, so it is best to eat them within a couple of weeks. Layer the sweets, without touching, in between layers of non-stick baking paper for best results. Pieces of toffee can be wrapped in small pieces of baking paper or cellophane if you like.

GIFT PACKAGING

If you are making sweets to give to friends and family, or even to sell, then it is nice to present them attractively. Small cellophane bags and sheets of cellophane are available from craft shops or online stores, and some florists will sell you a roll of cellophane at a good price. When making large quantities of sweets, it is sensible to store them in single layers in large boxes so that they do not stick together or get marked through contact or overhandling before you wrap them up. Always use a pair of disposable vinyl gloves when handling finished confectionery so that you do not mark it with fingerprints.

Clear bags, or for that matter, gift boxes, look lovely when wrapped and tied with ribbon – haberdashers or curtain shops often have short lengths of really lovely fabric ribbon that is much nicer than that available from supermarkets.

Remember that if you are giving someone a box of homemade chocolates, you might want to advise them to keep the box in a cool place if they are not going to open it straight away.

If you want to sell your confections, start by contacting your local trading standards and environmental health office for advice.

BOILED SWEETS AND TOFFEE

Toffees and hard, boiled confections such as humbugs are some of the simplest sweets to make, requiring few ingredients and little time. Most of our favourite boiled sweets are derived from simple sugar syrup, cooked to a specific temperature that means, when it has cooled, it will be hard and glass-like. Flavour and colour can be added as you choose, making it possible to make a seemingly endless variety.

The ability of sugar to form glass-like sweets and shapes has been understood for many centuries and yet, for most of recorded history, it was too expensive to be commonplace. Instead, jewelled fruits, sugar plates and models graced only the tables of the very wealthy. Sugar is now a relatively cheap ingredient, and so we can afford to experiment.

Toffee entered the world of sweets rather late compared to other boiled sweets. It seems to have grown in popularity at the same time that dairying as an art became more popular, in the 18th century – later than many of the simple nut and fruit sweets that had traditionally formed part of the dessert course at dinner.

Toffee recipes started to appear around the early part of the 19th century when toffee-making gatherings seem to have formed an excuse for winter parties, particularly in Wales and Scotland – which may be why we still associate it with bonfire night. Don't feel that you can only make toffee in the winter because it really is just as delicious for the rest of the year!

Recipes for toffee often contain an acid – lemon or vinegar, and butter – both of which help to prevent crystals forming in the hot liquid. Indeed, one of our most famous toffees, Everton, is very definitely a lemon-scented confection.

One major consideration should be remembered when working with sugar – although we can melt it into a clear, glass-like structure, it really loves to recrystallise. The Tips and Techniques on the following pages gives you all the advice needed for success.

TIPS AND TECHNIQUES

QUANTITIES AND PAN SIZES

Most of the recipes in this chapter use 500g–1kg ingredients which will be most effectively boiled in a medium to large saucepan of 16–20cm diameter, to hold 2–3 litres.

COOKING THE SUGAR SYRUP

All the sweets in this section begin with a sugar syrup made from water, sugar and usually additions of cream of tartar and glucose syrup to help prevent recrystallisation of the sugar, which would spoil the texture of your sweets.

Initially it is important to heat the mixture over a low heat, giving the sugar a chance to fully dissolve before the mixture boils. As a general rule I actually advise allowing the water or liquid to sit with the sugar in the pan for five minutes before applying any heat at all, as the sugar will start to dissolve gently this way. Otherwise it is tempting to rush the process and bring the syrup to a boil before the sugar is properly dissolved, which causes crystallisation later. It is best not to stir the syrup too vigorously as the sugar dissolves as this may leave stray crystals of sugar on the sides of the pan which might later on spoil the texture of your sweets – crystals are the enemy of the boiled sweet! If the sugar comes to the boil too soon, crystals will form in the syrup as it cooks.

Once the sugar has fully dissolved, raise the heat and bring the mixture to a boil. At this stage, monitor the temperature using a thermometer (see page 19). If using a gas hob, take care that the flames do not lick around the sides of the pan and caramelise or burn the syrup.

As the syrup cooks, you will notice that the temperature increases more quickly as the water evaporates. If your temperature probe has an alert system, set it for several degrees below your final temperature to give you time to prepare any trays or dishes that you need.

Arresting the heat

Temperature is always critical when making sweets, especially when cooking syrups to high temperatures as the syrup can easily overcook. It will help to fill your sink with an inch or two of cold water before starting, so you can dip the base of the pan in for a few seconds to arrest the cooking. Do not be tempted to stir the syrup to encourage it to cool because this will cause crystallisation and spoil your recipe.

Techniques used to prevent crystallisation

* Have a jug of hot water and pastry brush ready when boiling the syrup. Use it to brush the insides of the pan to prevent crystals from forming.

* Adding a pinch of cream of tartar to the sugar syrup at the start of cooking helps disrupt crystal formation.

* Some recipes use fat in the form of butter, cream or milk which disrupts, but does not prevent, crystal formation.

* Liquid glucose is used in some recipes and this alters the balance of the simple sugars in the mixture and so disrupts the formation of crystals.

POURING SUGAR SYRUP FOR TOFFEES

Toffee is usually poured and set in a shallow tray greased with a little butter. Pour the toffee in one go, and do not scrape the pan, otherwise you will risk the mixture crystallising.

PULLING BOILED SWEETS

When a boiled-sweet syrup is just made and poured for cooling, it is clear and, unless it is pulled, will remain clear and glass-like when cool. The technique of pulling causes the cooling syrup to turn opaque and 'satinise' – i.e. take on a satin-like sheen.

First, the hot syrup is poured onto a lightly oiled surface. A marble slab or granite surface is useful for this as it will cool the syrup quickly – if you have a clean stone worktop then you can use that. An alternative is a silicone non-stick baking mat set in a large baking tray. If you don't have a silicone mat, use a large baking tray lightly greased with oil.

The edges of the syrup cool quickly and must be turned over onto the centre of the syrup repeatedly using an oiled palette knife so that the mass cools evenly. This is repeated until the syrup is cool enough to handle. At this point, don some vinyl gloves and oil them lightly. Pull and fold the syrup back on itself repeatedly. As you do this, the syrup will thicken and turn opaque as air becomes trapped in it. When the 'syrup' is firm enough to hold its shape, it is rolled into its desired form and cut to the required size, be it a humbug or candy cane.

Safety note on handling hot sugar: Hot syrups will easily scald or burn if they come into contact with bare skin. Wear a long-sleeved shirt and sugar-work gloves or vinyl gloves to protect your skin at all times when cooking syrups. When making pulled sugar sweets, oil your gloves lightly and at first only use the tips of your fingers in case the sugar is still too hot.

COLOURING AND FLAVOURING

Striped boiled sweets are made by working two differently coloured portions of syrup until they are the same consistency, then folding or twisting them together depending on the result you desire. These sweets give you plenty of opportunity to experiment with flavours and colours.

CUTTING BOILED SWEETS AND TOFFEES

Boiled sweets such as humbugs are shaped by cutting a rope of coloured syrup into pillows or cushions. Bull's eyes are initially also shaped like this but are then rolled into balls. Use lightly oiled scissors to cut the hardened syrup, or chop using a large knife or metal scraper.

Toffees are more easily shaped using the blade of a knife to mark the cooling toffee into squares. It is then allowed to cool fully before it is dropped onto a clean board and broken along the marks.

Makes
6

SPUN SUGAR LOLLIPOPS

Pure strands of sugar result from this recipe – not as fine as candyfloss, but just as fun to eat. Make sure that no one else is in the kitchen when you are spinning the sugar as the molten confection will burn easily.

Time: 30 minutes

600g granulated sugar
200ml water
100g liquid glucose
Few drops flavouring of
  your choice
Food colouring of your
  choice (paste is best)
Sunflower or almond oil,
  for greasing

You'll also need
Temperature probe or
  sugar thermometer
6 x 20cm-long lollipop sticks
Clipped whisk (see below)
  or use a fork

Fill your sink with cold water as you will need to cool the base of the pan.

Place the sugar, water and liquid glucose in a medium to large pan and allow the sugar to start dissolving into the water for 5 minutes. Transfer the pan to a low heat and stir until the sugar is dissolved. Raise the heat and bring the mixture to the boil.

Stop stirring at this stage. Use a pastry brush dipped in hot water to brush down the sides of the pan to remove any sugar crystals.

Cook the mixture until the syrup reaches 155°C, then dip the base of the pan in the water-filled sink for a couple of seconds to arrest the cooking process. Transfer the pan onto a heatproof surface, add the flavouring and a tiny amount of your chosen colouring and stir these in briefly.

The syrup needs to cool a little before you will be able to use it – only a minute or two. Line your work surface and floor around where you are working with non-stick baking paper. Grease the handle of a wooden spoon with a little oil.

Dip the clipped whisk into the syrup and let any excess syrup drip back into the pan. Then, holding the spoon in one hand and the whisk in the other, swing the whisk back and forth over the spoon handle to produce strands of sugar syrup which will harden immediately. If the sugar is still too liquid and simply flies off, allow it to cool a little before trying again. However, if you find the sugar is thickening as you work, simply reheat gently over a low heat.

As soon as you have made enough for one lollipop stick, dip the tip of the stick in the hot syrup and attach a ball of the spun sugar to it. Continue until you have used up all of the sugar. Eat as soon as you can, as the strands will soon soften in a humid kitchen.

Make a clipped whisk by cutting the head of an old largish whisk using wire cutters or pliers so that you are left with straight pieces of wire about 15–20cm long attached to the handle. Or you can opt to use two large forks held back to back instead.

Makes
1 plate

SUGAR GLASS PLATE

Jewel-like shapes can be made easily with poured molten sugar. This plate is great fun to serve your desserts on, and in fact represents one of the earliest forms of sugar work that were popular in the Tudor court.

Time: 20 minutes

500g granulated sugar
200ml water
125g liquid glucose
Food colouring of your
  choice (paste is best)
Sunflower or almond oil,
  for greasing

You'll also need
Temperature probe or sugar
  thermometer
Modelling clay such as
  Plasticine

Fill your sink with an inch or two of cold water as you will need to cool the base of the pan.

Place the sugar, water and liquid glucose in a medium to large pan and allow the sugar to start dissolving into the water for 5 minutes.

Meanwhile, draw a 25cm circle on a sheet of non-stick baking paper and lightly oil the circle. Place the paper on a large board. Make a strip of Plasticine approximately 1cm thick that is long enough to go around the circumference of the circle you have drawn. Stick the lightly oiled Plasticine strip around the edge of the circle, making sure that there are no gaps – you now have your plate mould.

Transfer the pan to a low heat and stir until the sugar is dissolved. Raise the heat and bring the mixture to the boil.

Stop stirring at this stage. Use a pastry brush dipped in hot water to wash down the sides of the pan to remove any crystals of sugar.

Cook the mixture until the syrup reaches 155°C, then dip the base of the pan in the water-filled sink for a couple of seconds to arrest the cooking process. Transfer the pan to a heatproof surface and add a tiny amount of colouring but only stir it in very briefly so that the finished plate has attractive swirls. Pour the syrup onto the baking paper and tilt the tray so that the sugar covers the entire circle. Use a small, sharp knife to prick any bubbles and then leave the plate to set. When it is quite cold, remove the Plasticine and place the plate in an airtight container until you need to use it. The plate will keep for a couple of days.

Note: The glass plate may warp in warm conditions, so allow it to set on a large metal tray.

Makes
30

BARLEY SUGAR TWISTS

Isabella adds lemon to the traditional barley sugar recipe, which is one of the simplest boiled sweets cooked to a light caramel stage. Be sure to read the techniques section at the beginning of this chapter before starting and, if you can, recruit a friend to help with the final shaping.

Time: 3 hours

60g pearl barley
Juice and pared rind
 of ½ lemon
600ml water
Sunflower or almond
 oil, for greasing
500g granulated sugar

You'll also need
Large silicone non-stick
 baking mat
Temperature probe or
 sugar thermometer
Vinyl gloves

Set the silicone mat on a large baking tray, or grease a large baking tray with a little oil. Fill your sink with an inch or two of cold water as you will need to cool the base of the pan.

Place a large pan over a medium heat and add the barley, lemon rind and water. Bring the mixture to a simmer, making sure the heat is very low, cover with a lid. Simmer the barley very gently for 1½–2 hours. Let the mixture settle for 20 minutes then, using a ladle, remove some of the clear liquid from the top of the barley – you should be able to obtain about 280ml. While the mixture settles, lightly oil a pair of kitchen scissors and a palette knife.

Place the sugar in a large, clean saucepan, and add your barley water. Bring the mixture to a gentle simmer over a medium heat, stirring to dissolve the sugar. Then raise the heat to high and allow the mixture to boil rapidly. Use a pastry brush dipped in hot water to wash down the sides of the pan to dissolve any crystals of sugar that might form. Use a temperature probe to monitor the mixture, and cook until it reaches a steady 149°C. At this point, remove the pan from the heat, dip the base of the pan in the water-filled sink for a couple of seconds and then stand it on a heatproof surface. When the bubbling has subsided, pour the syrup onto the silicone mat. It will run a little, but will soon begin to set. Using the oiled palette knife, fold the edges of the pool into the centre so that you have a more or less rectangular piece of caramel.

At this point, put on your vinyl gloves and oil your gloved hands lightly.

Keep an eye on the syrup and when it is cool enough to handle, use an oiled pair of kitchen scissors to cut it into strips. Holding the strips at both ends, twist in opposite directions to form long twists. As soon as they are cool, pack into an airtight container or tin layered between sheets of non-stick baking paper.

Makes
60

BULL'S EYES

This striped and pulled lemon sweet was popular with Victorian journeymen confectioners, along with 'sugar sticks' and 'Nelson's buttons'. Read the techniques section at the beginning of this chapter before starting. It helps to have a friend on standby to help with the final shaping.

Time: 45 minutes

500g light brown or
   demerara sugar
125ml water
75g liquid glucose
¼ tsp cream of tartar
½ tsp lemon extract
Sunflower or almond oil, for
   greasing

You'll also need
Temperature probe or sugar
   thermometer
Large silicone non-stick
   baking mat (optional)
Vinyl gloves

Fill your sink with an inch or two of cold water as you will need to cool the base of the pan. Set your silicone mat onto a large baking tray, or lightly grease a large baking tray with oil. Have a palette knife ready, along with your flavouring.

Place the sugar, water, liquid glucose and cream of tartar in a large pan and allow the sugar to start dissolving into the water for 5 minutes. Transfer the pan to a low heat and stir until the sugar is dissolved. Raise the heat and bring the mixture to the boil.

Stop stirring at this stage. Use a pastry brush dipped in hot water to wash down the sides of the pan to remove any crystals of sugar.

Cook the mixture until the syrup reaches 149°C, then dip the base of the pan in the sink of cold water briefly to arrest the cooking process. Stand the pan on a heatproof surface. Pour the syrup onto the non-stick mat, and let it cool for 1 minute. Using the palette knife, separate the syrup into two portions, one twice the size of the other. To the smaller portion, add the lemon extract.

At this point, put on your vinyl gloves and oil your gloved hands lightly.

With one hand, begin to knead the lemon portion, turning the mixture carefully over on itself on the tray until the mixture is evenly combined, but do not over-mix – it should remain brown. Knead the other portion of the syrup as it cools until it is firm enough to handle. As soon as you can pick it up, pull and fold it repeatedly until it satinises (i.e. turns from clear and glass-like to white and satiny). At this point, form the opaque syrup into a sausage, then roll the lemon portion into a strand the same length and place on top of it. Roll the two portions together until they are twice their original length, then fold in two, so you have two brown strips. Repeat this action and then roll the striped syrup out to a diameter of about 1cm.

Using a pair of oiled scissors, cut the roll into short lengths, then roll each portion quickly to form even balls. Work quickly at this stage as the sweets will cool in no time. If the roll does set so you are no longer able to cut it, do not worry. Simply allow it to cool and then break it into small pieces with a hammer. Store the bull's eyes in an airtight container or tin soon as they are cold.

Makes
100

ACID LEMON DROPS

A combination of icing sugar and citric acid is used to give a delightful tang to the outside of these lovely sweets.

Time: 45 minutes

500g granulated sugar
125ml water
¼ tsp cream of tartar
1 tsp citric acid
Yellow food colouring (paste
  is best)
1 tsp lemon or orange
  extract
2 tbsp icing sugar mixed
  with ½ tsp citric acid, for
  dusting
Sunflower or almond oil, for
  greasing

You'll also need
Large silicone non-stick
  baking mat (optional)
Temperature probe or sugar
  thermometer
Vinyl gloves

Set your silicone mat on a large baking tray, or lightly grease a large tray with oil. Fill your sink with an inch or two of cold water as you will need to cool the base of the pan.

Place the sugar, water and cream of tartar in a large pan set on a low heat and cook, stirring to dissolve the sugar. Raise the heat to medium-high and cook the syrup until it reaches 148°C. While the mixture boils, use a pastry brush dipped in hot water to wash down the insides of the pan to prevent crystals forming.

When the syrup reaches the desired temperature, remove it from the heat and dip the base of the pan into the water-filled sink briefly to arrest the cooking. Transfer the pan to a heatproof surface and add a tiny amount of yellow colouring and the lemon or orange extract to the syrup, stirring quickly to mix. Pour the syrup onto the silicone mat.

Don the vinyl gloves and grease both your hands and a palette knife with a little oil. Use the palette knife to turn the cooling syrup over a couple of times and then as soon as it begins to hold its shape, use your fingers to knead it. Pull the mixture and fold it over on itself repeatedly until it stiffens and begins to turn opaque. Roll the mass into a long sausage and tease one end out to a 5mm diameter roll, then use a pair of oiled scissors to cut small pieces from it. They will cool and set almost instantly. When you have used up all of the mixture, dust them with the icing sugar and citric acid mixture. Store in an airtight container or tin.

Makes
40

MINT CANDIES

A very simple sweet, with a clean fresh taste derived from using just fresh milk and sugar, and flavoured with peppermint extract.

Time: 35 minutes

500g granulated sugar
150ml fresh whole milk
1 tsp peppermint extract

You'll also need
Temperature probe or sugar
  thermometer

Line a large baking tray with non-stick baking paper.

Place the sugar and milk in a large pan and allow the sugar to start dissolving into the milk for 5 minutes. Transfer the pan to a low heat and stir until the sugar is dissolved.

Raise the heat to medium-high. Allow the mixture to boil, stirring occasionally. Use the pastry brush dipped in water to wash down the insides of the pan to prevent crystals forming which would otherwise spoil your recipe. Cook the mixture until it reaches 120°C, then remove from the heat and stand the pan on a heatproof surface or mat.

Add the peppermint extract, then beat the mixture with the whisk until it begins to form large crystals and goes stiff – this can take 5–10 minutes depending on how vigorously you beat.

Use a teaspoon to form the mixture into rough balls and set them on the prepared baking tray to cool. When cold, store in an airtight container or tin.

Makes
50

SHERBET FRUIT DROPS

Sherbet first appeared as a fortified, citrus-scented drink. The acid tang of the original drink is all that remains in modern sherbets, which derive their fizz from bicarbonate of soda.

Time: 45 minutes

500g granulated sugar
100g liquid glucose
125ml water
¼ tsp cream of tartar
1 tsp citric acid
Yellow, red and blue food
  colouring (paste is best)
Lemon, raspberry and
  lavender extracts
2 tbsp icing sugar mixed
  with ½ tsp bicarbonate of
  soda, for dusting
Sunflower or almond oil, for
  greasing

You'll also need
Large silicone non-stick
  baking mat (optional)
Temperature probe or sugar
  thermometer
Vinyl gloves

Set your non-stick baking mat on a large baking tray or lightly grease a large baking tray with oil. Fill your sink with an inch or two of cold water as you will need to cool the base of the pan.

Place the sugar, liquid glucose, water and cream of tartar in a large pan set on a low heat and cook, stirring to dissolve the sugar. Raise the heat to medium-high and cook the syrup until it reaches 148°C. While the mixture boils, use a pastry brush dipped in hot water to wash down the insides of the pan to prevent crystals forming.

When the syrup reaches the desired temperature, remove it from the heat and dip the base of the pan into the water-filled sink briefly to arrest the cooking.

Transfer the pan to a heatproof surface and add the citric acid. Pour the syrup onto the non-stick mat. Don the vinyl gloves and grease both your hands and a palette knife with a little oil.

Use the palette knife to turn the cooling syrup over a couple of times and then, as soon as it begins to hold its shape, divide the syrup into three equal parts. Colour and flavour each portion with a tiny amount of colouring and flavouring (try 2–3 drops of colouring for a start – you can always add more).

Knead each portion to mix the colour in fully. Take care to wash your hands between each colour.

Knead each portion in turn until the syrup will form a soft roll. Pile the three portions on top of each other, having made sure that they are roughly the same shape and length. Gently press the three portions together and roll the cooling syrup on the mat until you have an even roll about 1cm in diameter.

Use oiled scissors to snip the roll into short lengths or triangles, scattering them over the mat so that they cool quickly and do not stick to one another. Toss the finished sweets in the mixture of icing sugar and bicarbonate of soda. When fully cold, store in an airtight container or tin.

Makes
60

ANISEED HUMBUGS

The simple humbug developed, like many strongly flavoured sweets, from early remedies for colds and coughs. You should read the techniques section at the beginning of this chapter before starting. It helps to have a friend to hand for the final shaping.

Time: 40 minutes

500g granulated sugar
125ml water
¼ tsp cream of tartar
Black food colouring (paste is best)
½ tsp aniseed or mint extract
Sunflower or almond oil, for greasing

You'll also need
Large silicone non-stick baking mat (optional)
Temperature probe or sugar thermometer
Vinyl gloves

Fill your sink with an inch or two of cold water as you will need to cool the base of the pan. Put your silicone mat onto a large baking tray, or lightly grease a large baking tray with oil. Have a palette knife ready, along with colouring and flavouring.

Place the sugar, water and cream of tartar in a large pan and stir well for 5 minutes to dissolve the sugar. Turn the heat down to low and stir until the sugar is completely dissolved. Turn the heat up and bring the mixture to the boil.

Stop stirring at this stage. Use a pastry brush dipped in hot water to wash down the sides of the pan to remove any crystals of sugar.

Cook the mixture until the syrup reaches 149°C, then dip the base of the pan into the water-filled sink for a couple of seconds to arrest the cooking process. Stand the pan on a heatproof surface. Pour the syrup onto the silicone mat, and let it cool for 1 minute. Using the palette knife, separate the syrup into two portions, one twice the size of the other. To the smaller portion, add a tiny amount of black colouring. To the other, add the aniseed extract. At this point, put on your vinyl gloves and oil your gloved hands lightly.

With one hand, begin to fold the black portion together, turning the mixture carefully over and over on itself on the tray, kneading the syrup until the mixture is evenly coloured. Wash your gloved hands to remove any trace of colour. Knead the other portion of the syrup as it cools until it is firm enough to handle – and as soon as you can pick it up, knead it until it satinises (i.e. turns from clear and glass-like to white and satiny). At this point, form the white syrup into a sausage and roll the black portion into a strand the same length. Place one on top of the other and roll the two colours together until they are twice their original length, then fold in two. Repeat this action, so you have four black strips, and then roll the striped syrup out to a diameter of approximately 1cm.

Using a pair of oiled scissors, cut the roll into short lengths – they will form the traditional cushion shape. Work quickly at this stage as the sweets will cool quickly. If the roll does set so you are no longer able to cut it, do not worry. Simply allow it to cool and then break it into small pieces with a hammer. Store the humbugs in an airtight container or tin as soon as they are cold.

Makes
10

EDINBURGH ROCK

This traditional sweet was sold in boxes printed with the Ferguson or Royal Stewart tartan. Rock has a special and unique texture, very different to other boiled sweets, which are more glass-like. Rock, on the other hand, is crumbly or, rather, powdery – and delicious. It can be flavoured and coloured as you like.

Time: 35 minutes

500g granulated sugar
1 tbsp liquid glucose
200ml water
¼ tsp cream of tartar
Blue or green food colouring
  (paste is best)
½ tsp peppermint extract
Icing sugar, for dusting

You'll also need
Large silicone non-stick
  baking mat (optional)
Temperature probe or sugar
  thermometer
Vinyl gloves

Fill your sink with an inch or two of cold water as you will need to cool the base of the pan. Put your silicone mat onto a large baking tray or lightly grease a large baking tray with oil.

Place the sugar, liquid glucose, water and cream of tartar in a medium to large pan and allow the sugar to start dissolving into the water for 5 minutes. Transfer the pan to a low heat and stir until the sugar is dissolved. Raise the heat to medium-high and bring the mixture to the boil. Stop stirring at this stage. Use a pastry brush dipped in hot water to wash down the sides of the pan to remove any crystals of sugar.

Cook the mixture until the syrup reaches 135°C, then dip the base of the pan in the water-filled sink for a few seconds to arrest the cooking process. Stand the pan on a heatproof surface. Pour the syrup onto the sheet, and let it cool for 1 minute. Using the palette knife, separate the syrup into two portions, one twice the size of the other. To the smaller portion, add a tiny amount of green or blue food colouring. To the other, add the peppermint extract.

At this point, put on your vinyl gloves and oil your hands lightly.

With one hand, begin to fold the blue or green portion together, turning the mixture carefully over and over on itself on the tray, kneading the syrup until evenly coloured. Wash your gloved hands to remove any trace of colour. Knead the other portion of the syrup as it cools until it is firm enough to handle – and as soon as you can pick it up, knead it until it satinises (i.e. turns from clear and glass-like to white and satiny) – this can take up to 10 minutes. At this point, form the white syrup into a sausage. Press the green or blue portion into a sheet the same length and place the white piece on top of it. Roll the two colours together until they form a roll of white covered with green or blue, about 1–1.5cm in diameter.

Dust the rock with a little icing sugar, and using a pair of oiled scissors, cut the roll into 10cm lengths and continue to roll these gently as they cool. Leave the rock at room temperature overnight to soften. Store in a cool dry place.

Makes
30

ROSE CANDY CANES

Rose and other flower extracts are very widely used in confectionery, and these striped twists are a very old-fashioned fairground treat. Traditionally, boiled sugar mixtures would often be moulded into the shape of a shepherd's crook or walking cane, or perhaps cut to mimic the shape of a cockscomb.

Time: 30 minutes

500g granulated sugar
100g liquid glucose
125ml water
¼ tsp cream of tartar
Red food colouring
  (paste is best)
½ tsp rose extract
Sunflower or almond oil,
  for greasing

You'll also need
Large silicone non-stick
  baking mat (optional)
Temperature probe or
  sugar thermometer
Vinyl gloves

Set the silicone mat on a large baking tray or lightly grease a large baking tray with oil. Fill your sink with an inch or two of cold water as you will need to cool the base of the pan.

Place the sugar, liquid glucose, water and cream of tartar in a medium to large pan and allow the sugar to start dissolving into the water for 5 minutes. Transfer the pan to a low heat and stir until the sugar is dissolved. Turn the heat up and bring to the boil.

Stop stirring at this stage. Use a pastry brush dipped in hot water to wash down the sides of the pan to remove any crystals of sugar.

Cook the mixture until the syrup reaches 149°C, then dip the base of the pan in the water-filled sink to arrest the cooking process. Stand the pan on a heatproof surface. Pour the syrup onto the sheet, and let it cool for 1 minute. Using the palette knife, separate the syrup into two portions, one twice the size of the other. To the smaller portion, add a tiny amount of red food colouring. To the other, add the rose extract.

At this point, put on your vinyl gloves and oil your hands lightly.

With one hand, begin to fold the red portion together, turning the mixture carefully over and over on itself on the tray, kneading the syrup until the mixture is evenly coloured. Wash your gloved hands to remove any trace of colour. Knead the other portion of the syrup as it cools until it is firm enough to handle – and as soon as you can pick it up, knead it until it satinises (i.e. turns from clear and glass-like to white and satiny). At this point, form the white syrup into a sausage, then roll the red portion into a strand the same length and place on top of it. Roll the two colours together until they are twice their original length, then fold in two, so you have two red strips. Repeat this action and then roll the striped syrup out to a diameter of about 5mm. Using a pair of oiled scissors, cut the roll into 10cm lengths and continue to roll these gently as they cool. Turn one end of each piece back to form the shape of a shepherd's crook or walking stick. Allow the pieces to cool and set, then store them in an airtight container.

Makes
20–30

STRIPY ST CLEMENT'S LOLLIPOPS

Sharp and zingy, these two-tone lollipops are fun to make, and you can vary the flavours and colours to suit your liking. Of course, like the nursery rhyme, they really should be flavoured like 'oranges and lemons'.

Time: 30 minutes
—

500g granulated sugar
125ml water
¼ tsp cream of tartar
1 tsp citric acid
½ teaspoon orange extract
1 teaspoon lemon extract
Yellow and orange food
  colouring (paste is best)

You'll also need
30 lollipop sticks
Temperature probe or
  sugar thermometer
Funnel (optional)

Arrange several baking trays and line them with non-stick baking paper. Place the lollipop sticks on them, spacing them 10cm or so apart. Fill your sink with an inch or two of cold water as you will need to cool the base of the pan.

Place the sugar, water and cream of tartar in a large pan set on a low heat and stir to dissolve the sugar. Raise the heat to medium-high and cook the syrup until it reaches 148°C. While the mixture boils, use a pastry brush to wash down the insides of the pan to prevent crystals forming.

When the syrup reaches the desired temperature, remove it from the heat and dip the base of the pan into the water-filled sink to arrest the cooking. Add the citric acid to the pan, stir briefly to mix, and transfer the pan to a heatproof surface. Pour one-third of the syrup into a heatproof bowl or small pan and add a tiny amount of orange colouring and the orange extract, stirring quickly to mix. Add a tiny amount of yellow colouring and the lemon extract to the remaining syrup, mixing quickly.

Use a teaspoon to drop a small pool of orange syrup onto the tip of each stick until you have used it all up. To finish the lollies, place the funnel in a measuring jug and sit the handle of a wooden spoon in the funnel to block it. Pour the lemon syrup into the funnel, creating a dispenser for the lollies.

Working quickly, hold the funnel over the tip of a stick with one hand and lift the wooden spoon briefly to allow a pool of syrup to form around the orange pool, leaving no gaps. Repeat until you have used up all the syrup. (If you haven't got a funnel, or if your funnel blocks, you can also use a small ladle or large spoon to create the same effect.)

Allow the lollies to cool briefly before wrapping in cellophane, or layering in an airtight container or tin between sheets of non-stick baking paper.

Makes
20–30

STRAWBERRY LOLLIPOPS

This recipe uses real fruit juice to create a chewy fruit sweet. It involves work over two separate days, so plan ahead.

Time: 30 minutes plus
  overnight freezing and
  draining

300g strawberries
500g granulated sugar
¼ tsp cream of tartar
½ tsp citric acid

You'll also need
30 lollipop sticks
Temperature probe or
  sugar thermometer
Funnel (optional)

Wash the berries and allow them to dry on a clean tea towel. Place the berries in a large bowl with 1 tablespoon of the sugar. Mash the strawberries completely, and tip them into a colander lined with muslin set over a large bowl. Place a sheet of cling film over the top and allow the juice to drain overnight in a cool place.

When you have gathered 125–150ml strawberry juice, transfer it to a pan with the sugar, cream of tartar and citric acid. If you have not got enough juice, make up the volume with clear apple juice.

Line several baking trays with non-stick baking paper. Arrange the trays on your kitchen worktop and place the lollipop sticks on them, spacing them 10cm or so apart.

Place the pan on a low heat and cook, stirring to dissolve the sugar. Raise the heat to medium-high and cook the syrup until it reaches 143°C. While the mixture boils, use a pastry brush dipped in hot water to wash down the insides of the pan to prevent crystals forming.

To make the lollies, place the funnel in a measuring jug and sit the handle of a wooden spoon in the funnel to block it. Pour some of the syrup into the funnel, creating a dispenser for the lollies. Working quickly, hold the funnel over the tip of a lollipop stick with one hand and lift the wooden spoon briefly to allow a pool of syrup to form around the tip of each stick, which should be central to the pool. Repeat until you have used up all the syrup. (If you haven't got a funnel, you can also use a small ladle or large spoon to create the same effect.)

When the lollies are set and cold, wrap each one in non-stick baking paper or cellophane and store in an airtight container.

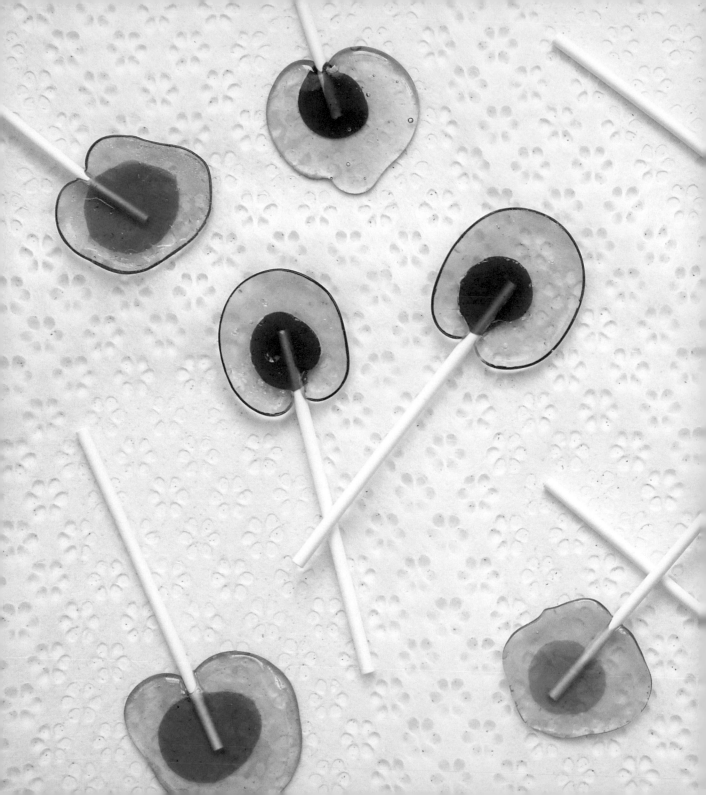

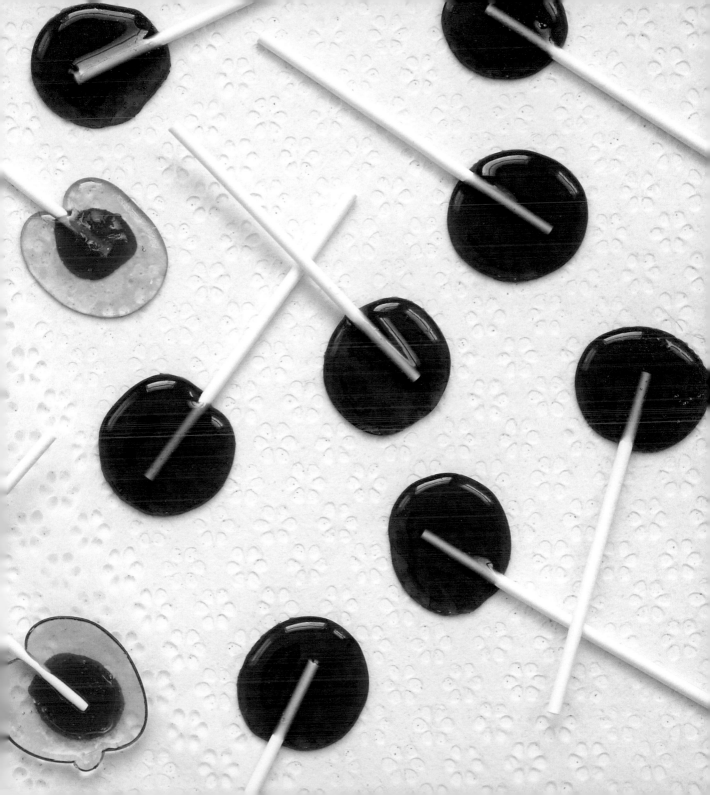

Makes about 550g

DARK TREACLE TOFFEE

Treacle and molasses are almost bitter tasting and either can be used here to make a delicious dark toffee. Pay particular attention to the mixture as it cooks because it burns easily. If you prefer, you can pour the cooked toffee onto a non-stick mat, allow it to cool for a few minutes and then pull it into ropes before cutting it into lengths to create treacle sticks.

Time: 25 minutes

250g black treacle or
  molasses
250g dark muscovado sugar
1 tsp lemon juice
25ml water
60g butter
Pinch of salt
Butter or sunflower oil,
  for greasing

You'll also need
Baking tin, roughly
  20cm-square
Temperature probe or sugar
  thermometer

Grease the baking tin with a little butter or sunflower oil.

Place the ingredients in a large pan and heat gently until the butter has melted and the sugar has dissolved. Increase the heat and then boil, stirring frequently until the mixture reaches 143°C. While the toffee boils, use a pastry brush dipped in hot water to wash down the insides of the pan to prevent any sugar crystals forming.

When the mixture is up to temperature pour the toffee into the prepared tin. Allow the toffee to cool fully, then tip the toffee out onto a clean chopping board and use a toffee hammer to smash the toffee into pieces. Store the toffee in an airtight container or tin.

Makes
48

EVERTON TOFFEE

Isabella gave a lovely recipe for this traditional toffee, but quite why Everton became renowned for its toffee we may never know. Make sure you do not stir the toffee at all when it has reached its temperature otherwise it will lose its glass-like texture.

Time: 20 minutes

500g demerara or
 granulated sugar
125g salted butter
300ml water
½ tsp lemon extract
Butter or sunflower oil,
 for greasing

You'll also need
Baking tin, roughly
 20 x 30cm
Temperature probe or sugar
 thermometer

Grease the baking tin with a little butter or sunflower oil.

Place the ingredients in a large pan and heat gently until the butter has melted and the sugar has dissolved. Increase the heat and then boil, stirring frequently until the mixture reaches 145°C. While the toffee boils, use a pastry brush dipped in hot water to wash down the insides of the pan to prevent any sugar crystals forming.

When the mixture is up to temperature, add the lemon extract, leave it to bubble for 30 seconds, and then pour the toffee into the prepared tin. Allow the toffee to cool for an hour or so, then mark it into squares with a sharp knife – 2–3cm squares is about right. Cool fully, then tip the tin out onto a clean tray. Store the toffees in an airtight container or tin.

Makes
48

BUTTERSCOTCH

Thought to originate in Yorkshire, the name derives not from any place of origin, but from the way that the cooked mixture is cut, or 'scotched', into small squares. Isabella recommends using brown sugar and flavouring with dried ginger to help with coughs.

Time: 20 minutes

500g muscovado or
  granulated sugar
140ml double cream
150ml water
¼ tsp cream of tartar
90g salted butter, plus a little
  extra for greasing
½ tsp ground ginger

You'll also need
15cm-square baking tin
Temperature probe or sugar
  thermometer

Grease the baking tin with a little butter.

Place the ingredients in a large pan and heat gently until the butter has melted and the sugar has dissolved. Increase the heat and then boil, stirring frequently until the mixture reaches 138°C. While the mixture boils, use a pastry brush dipped in hot water to wash down the insides of the pan to prevent any sugar crystals forming.

When the mixture is up to temperature pour the butterscotch into the prepared tin. Allow the toffee to cool for an hour or so, then mark it into squares with a sharp knife – 2–3cm squares is about right. Cool fully, then tip the tin out onto a clean tray. Store in an airtight container or tin.

Makes
8

BONFIRE TOFFEE APPLES

This recipe uses a slightly richer toffee than Isabella's Everton recipe to wrap around dessert apples — which are great fun for children on bonfire night or indeed at any other time of year.

Time: 30 minutes

8 medium Cox's Orange
  Pippin apples (or other
  sharp and aromatic eating
  apples)
40g salted butter, plus extra
  for greasing
350g soft brown sugar
125ml water
1 tsp lemon juice
170g golden syrup

You'll also need
8 x 15cm long lollipop sticks
  or pieces of dowel
Temperature probe or sugar
  thermometer
Clear cellophane (optional)

Wash the apples in very hot water to remove any wax and dry well. Spear the stalk end of each apple with a lollipop stick. Grease a baking tray and prepare a jug of very cold water large enough to dip an apple into. Set both aside.

Place the rest of the ingredients into a large pan over a medium heat and allow them to melt together, then turn the heat to high and bring the mixture to the boil. Stir constantly and use a temperature probe to monitor the syrup. It is ready when it reaches approximately 148°C.

Working quickly before the toffee sets, hold an apple by the stick and dip it into the toffee, swirling it to ensure it is completely covered. Lift it out of the mixture, allow it to drip for a few seconds and then plunge it into the jug of water and set it, with the stick pointing upwards, on the prepared baking tray. Repeat the process with the remaining apples. Leave them to cool for 10 minutes, then wrap each apple in cellophane or non-stick baking paper.

Makes
400g

TOFFEE POPCORN CLUSTERS

American confections began to find their way into the British kitchen in the late 19th century with fudge and cream caramels being popular. Here, a simple toffee is used to glaze freshly popped corn for a TV treat.

Time: 20 minutes

150g popcorn
300g demerara sugar
25g salted butter
70ml water
Seeds from 1 vanilla pod
Sunflower oil, for greasing

You'll also need
Temperature probe or sugar
   thermometer

Line a large baking tray with non-stick baking paper. Lightly grease a silicone spatula or wooden spoon with sunflower oil.

Pop your popcorn according to the instructions on the packet. Set aside.

Put the sugar, butter, water and vanilla seeds in a large saucepan and simmer the ingredients over a low heat until the sugar is dissolved. Raise the heat to medium-high and bring the mixture to the boil. Use a pastry brush dipped in hot water to wash down the insides of the pan to prevent any sugar crystals forming. When the toffee has reached 124–126°C, remove the pan from the heat.

Spread the popcorn out on the baking tray and pour the syrup over it. Use the spatula or wooden spoon to mix the popcorn and toffee together, then allow it to cool in small chunks. When it is cold, store in an airtight container or tin for up to 10 days.

CARAMEL & FUDGE

Caramel and fudge are derived from very similar ingredients, but it is largely the way that the cooked mixtures are handled which gives their individual characteristics. Caramel is not stirred at all during cooking, so that no sugar crystals develop, and it is left to cool undisturbed to produce a sheer, chewy texture. Fruit purées, or indeed salt, can be added to caramel to balance the richness of all that cream.

Fudge is cooked to a relatively low temperature compared to caramels and toffees, and requires a certain degree of patience as, once cooked, it must be cooled before beating to produce a specific texture. The result is well worth it, however, and the crystallisation process can be carefully controlled to give the texture you desire (see overleaf).

Fudge is thought to have originated in the late 19th century when it was popular as a confection in east coast colleges in the US. Similar soft candies exist elsewhere such as Mexico and India and may have acted as precursors to modern fudge, but it is unlikely that Isabella ever tasted fudge, which was developed after her early death. Caramels derive largely from the tradition of toffee making, with additional cream or dairy products to provide a little luxury.

When cooked to a high temperature, the proteins present in milk and cream break down into delicious aromatic chemicals which give fudge and caramel utterly delicious flavours that will make you want to try the recipes in this chapter over and over again.

TIPS AND TECHNIQUES

PAN SIZES

Most of the caramel recipes in this chapter use 0.75–1.5kg of ingredients, which will be most effectively boiled in a large saucepan of 20–30cm diameter, to hold 3–4 litres. The majority of fudge recipes use 1–2kg of ingredients for which the same size pan can be used.

CARAMEL TECHNIQUES

Caramel requires less work than fudge; there is no stirring or beating involved because the confection is poured into a lined tin or mould as soon as it reaches the right temperature – around 120–125°C. Caramels have a particularly sheer, smooth texture which would be ruined by the presence of sugar crystals. For this reason, a pastry brush and a jug of hot water are required so that you can brush down the insides of the pan as the caramel cooks so that no crystals form as it cooks.

Fruit caramels

Caramels can have fruit purées added to lighten their flavour and vary the standard mixture of sugar, butter and cream. The best fruits to use have strong, lightly acidic flavours such as raspberry, passionfruit and blackcurrant. Soft bland fruits such as strawberry and blueberry work less well. It is better to use ripe, fully flavoured fruit for the best flavour, and not sweetened juices.

FUDGE TECHNIQUES

Everyone has their favourite texture and flavour of fudge. Whereas some prefer a yielding, fine fudge, others like it crumbly and crystalline. The good news is that each recipe in this chapter can be made either way – the key to success with fudge is in the way that it is handled as it cools.

Because fudge burns easily, you will find it safer to only cook the mixture over a medium heat rather than high. Fudge is typically cooked to 116°C, and is stirred only occasionally to prevent the mixture burning. During the cooking process, care must be taken to use a wet pastry brush to wash down the insides of the pan immediately above the boiling mixture to prevent crystals forming too early in the process. Once the fudge reaches the desired temperature, the base of the pan should be briefly dipped in a sink filled with cold water to prevent it overcooking.

For crumbly, crystalline fudge

Beat the cooked fudge immediately after arresting the cooking process. At this high temperature, the sugar crystals form quickly and are large. Beat until the fudge is nearly too stiff to pour, then pour it quickly into the prepared tin, smooth the surface and leave the fudge to cool fully before cutting.

For perfectly smooth fudge

Do not stir the fudge at all after it is cooked. Arrest the cooking process as described above, stand the pan on a heatproof mat and allow the fudge to cool to between 50 and 70°C. If your temperature probe has an alarm function, you will find it handy to use this so you can get on with another job. Beat the fudge either with a large hand whisk or with an electric mixer until it thickens and is evenly smooth, then press it into your prepared tin. Cut the fudge when fully cold.

Occasionally when beating the cooled fudge, you may notice that the mixture releases oils, or appears to split. Don't let this worry you, simply continue to beat the mixture and, as it cools, the oil will be reabsorbed.

Makes
2 x 400ml
jars

SOFT SALTED CARAMEL

Use this soft salted caramel as a filling for cakes, topping for ice cream or for the Chocolate Hazelnut Salted Caramels on page 170.

Time: 35 minutes

420g granulated sugar
110ml water
200ml double cream or
  crème fraiche
300g unsalted butter
6g sea salt flakes (preferably
  Maldon)
Seeds from 2 vanilla pods

You'll also need
Temperature probe or
  sugar thermometer

Place the sugar and water in a medium pan set on a low heat and cook, stirring, until the sugar has dissolved. Increase the heat to medium-high and allow the mixture to boil without stirring. As the syrup cooks, use a pastry brush dipped in water to wash down the insides of the pan to prevent any crystals forming. Cook the syrup until it turns first to a light yellow, then mid-brown caramel, and stop when the syrup reaches 165°C. Add the cream to the pan, and stir until the mixture is smooth and even, then add the butter, salt and vanilla seeds. Stir the mixture occasionally as it cools.

Store in the fridge in an airtight container or jar when fully cold.

Makes
40–50

CARAMEL LOLLIPOPS

These lollies make a real treat for a party. Many craft shops sell lollipop sticks, but you can also order them online – see the Suppliers section on page 202.

Time: 45 minutes

400g granulated sugar
240g golden syrup
20ml water
120ml double cream
Seeds from 1 vanilla pod
170g unsalted butter

You'll also need
Lollipop sticks
Temperature probe or
   sugar thermometer
Funnel (optional)

Lay out several baking trays and line them with non-stick baking paper. Place the lollipop sticks on them, spacing them 10cm or so apart.

Place the sugar, golden syrup and water in a medium pan set on a low heat and cook. Stir until the sugar has dissolved.

Increase the heat to medium-high and allow the mixture to boil without stirring. As the caramel cooks, use a pastry brush dipped in water to wash down the insides of the pan to prevent any crystals forming. Cook the mixture until it reaches 154°C.

While the caramel cooks, heat the cream and vanilla seeds in a small pan, and when the caramel is up to temperature remove it from the heat and add the cream carefully so as not to scald yourself. Add the butter and let it melt. Return the mixture to the heat and allow it to boil until it reaches 145°C.

To make the lollies, place the funnel in a measuring jug and sit the handle of a wooden spoon in the funnel to block it. Pour some of the caramel mixture into the funnel, creating a dispenser for the lollies. Working quickly, hold the funnel over the tip of a lollipop stick with one hand and lift the wooden spoon briefly to allow a pool of caramel to form around the tip of the stick – this should be central to the pool. Repeat until you have used up all the caramel. (If you haven't got a funnel, or if your funnel blocks, you can also use a small ladle or large spoon to create the same effect.)

When the lollies are set and cold, wrap each one in non-stick baking paper or cellophane and store in an airtight container.

Makes
80

HARD CARAMELS

This recipe produces a hard caramel, which resembles a luxurious toffee. Take great care to stir the mixture constantly because it has a tendency to burn above 113°C.

Time: 1 hour plus
  overnight cooling

400ml double cream
350ml milk
250g granulated sugar
120g demerara sugar
375g liquid glucose
300g unsalted butter
Seeds from 1 vanilla pod
Pinch salt

You'll also need
18cm-square baking tin
Temperature probe or sugar
  thermometer

Line the baking tin with non-stick baking paper.

Place all the ingredients in a large pan set on a low heat and cook. Stir until the sugar has dissolved and the butter has melted.

Increase the heat to medium-high and allow the mixture to boil without stirring.

As the caramel cooks, use a pastry brush dipped in water to wash down the insides of the pan to prevent any crystals forming. Stir the mixture constantly when the heat passes 113°C, making sure you scrape the bottom of the pan as you do to prevent the mixture burning.

As soon as the caramel has reached 121°C, immediately remove it from the heat and pour into the prepared tin. Prick out any air bubbles with the tip of a sharp knife and allow the mixture to cool fully in a dry place overnight. The next day, break the caramel into small squares and wrap in pieces of non-stick baking paper.

Makes
48

BLACK TREACLE CARAMELS

The addition of black treacle to a traditional caramel recipe lends a degree of bitterness that treacle fans will love. The sweets are sticky, dark and gloriously silky.

Time: 35 minutes plus
  overnight cooling

—

380ml double cream
400g granulated sugar
240ml black treacle
55g unsalted butter
Pinch sea salt

You'll also need
18cm-square baking tin
Temperature probe or sugar
  thermometer

Line the baking tin with non-stick baking paper.

Place all the ingredients in a large pan set on a low heat and cook. Stir until the sugar has dissolved and the butter has melted.

Increase the heat to medium-high and allow the mixture to boil without stirring. As the caramel cooks, use a pastry brush dipped in water to wash down the insides of the pan to prevent any crystals forming.

As soon as the caramel has reached 121°C, immediately remove it from the heat and pour into the prepared tin. Prick out any air bubbles with the tip of a sharp knife and allow the mixture to cool fully in a dry place overnight. The next day, cut the caramel into small squares and wrap in pieces of non-stick baking paper.

Makes
48

SALTED CARAMELS

Caramels are enriched with cream, butter and sugar and are cooked to a tender, silky confection.
A light touch of sea salt provides a lovely contrast to these caramels, which are traditionally made on
the Brittany coast.

Time: 35 minutes plus
  overnight cooling
———
380ml double cream
400g granulated sugar
240ml golden syrup
55g unsalted butter
Seeds from 1 vanilla pod
15g sea salt flakes
  (preferably Maldon)

You'll also need
24 x 18cm baking tray
Temperature probe or
  sugar thermometer

Line the baking tray with non-stick baking paper.

Place the ingredients, but only half the salt, in a large pan set on a low heat and cook, stirring, until the sugar has dissolved and the butter has melted. Increase the heat to medium-high and allow the mixture to boil without stirring. As the caramel cooks, use a pastry brush dipped in water to wash down the insides of the pan to prevent any crystals forming.

As soon as the caramel has reached 121°C, immediately remove it from the heat and pour into the prepared tin. Prick out any air bubbles with the tip of a sharp knife, sprinkle over the remaining salt, and allow the mixture to cool fully in a dry place overnight. The next day, cut the caramel into small squares and wrap in pieces of non-stick baking paper.

Makes
48

CHOCOLATE CARAMELS

This recipe combines two delicious flavours and the result is incredibly rich, so cut the pieces quite small once the caramel is cold enough to handle.

Time: 35 minutes plus
overnight cooling

100g granulated sugar
100g muscovado sugar
60g golden syrup
130g best-quality dark
chocolate, chopped into
small pieces
240ml double cream
20g salted butter
seeds from ½ vanilla pod
125ml water

You'll also need
18cm-square baking tin
Temperature probe or sugar
thermometer

Line the baking tin with non-stick baking paper.

Place all the ingredients into a large pan set on a low heat. Stir until the sugar has dissolved and the butter and chocolate have melted.

Increase the heat to medium-high and allow the mixture to boil without stirring. As the caramel cooks, use a pastry brush dipped in water to wash down the insides of the pan to prevent any crystals forming.

As soon as the caramel has reached 121°C, immediately remove it from the heat and pour into the prepared tin. Prick out any air bubbles with the tip of a sharp knife and allow the mixture to cool fully in a dry place overnight. The next day, cut the caramel into small squares and wrap in pieces of non-stick baking paper.

Makes
48

COFFEE CARAMELS

Although the first coffee house in England opened in 1650, many 19th century writers still felt the need to give precise recipes for its brewing. Isabella mentions that two French coffee houses roast their beans with butter and sugar – hence this new recipe for coffee caramels.

Time: 45 minutes plus
  overnight cooling
—

50g muscovado sugar
300g granulated sugar
60ml golden syrup
240ml double cream
55g unsalted butter
Pinch sea salt flakes
  (preferably Maldon)
1 tsp coffee extract or 2
  tsp instant coffee powder,
  dissolved in 1 tsp hot
  water

You'll also need
24 x 18cm baking tray
Temperature probe or sugar
  thermometer

Line the baking tray with non-stick baking paper.

Place the ingredients in a large pan set on a low heat. Stir until the sugar has dissolved and the butter has melted.

Increase the heat to medium-high and allow the mixture to boil without stirring.

As the caramel cooks, use a pastry brush dipped in water to wash down the insides of the pan to prevent any crystals forming.

As soon as the caramel has reached 121°C, immediately remove it from the heat and pour Into the prepared tin. Prick out any air bubbles with the tip of a sharp knife and allow the mixture to cool fully in a dry place overnight. The next day, cut the caramel into small squares and wrap in pieces of non-stick baking paper.

Makes
64

RASPBERRY CARAMELS

Fruit juices were regularly extracted and used for jellies and pastes in Isabella's kitchen. Adding fresh fruit juice to a cream-based caramel results in a pleasant light flavour as this recipe illustrates.

Time: 45 minutes plus
 overnight cooling

120ml double cream
200g unsalted butter
250g raspberries, sieved, to
 yield 200g purée
400g granulated sugar
200g demerara sugar

You'll also need
24 x 18cm baking tray
Temperature probe or
 sugar thermometer

Line the baking tray with non-stick baking paper.

Place the ingredients in a large pan set on a low heat and cook. Stir until the sugar has dissolved and the butter has melted.

Increase the heat to medium-high and allow the mixture to boil without stirring. As the caramel cooks, use a pastry brush dipped in water to wash down the insides of the pan to prevent any crystals forming.

As soon as the caramel has reached 121°C, immediately remove it from the heat and pour into the prepared tin. Prick out any air bubbles with the tip of a sharp knife and allow the mixture to cool fully in a dry place overnight. The next day, cut the caramel into small squares and wrap in pieces of non-stick baking paper.

Makes
64

BLACKCURRANT LIQUORICE CARAMELS

Liquorice production in Britain centered on Pontefract and the town still has an annual festival to celebrate this unusual plant. Liquorice powder can be found in Indian or continental grocers. If you cannot find it, use aniseed extract, which has a similar flavour.

Time: 45 minutes plus
  overnight cooling

200g blackcurrants
100ml water
120ml double cream
200g unsalted butter
400g granulated sugar
200g demerara sugar
¼ tsp liquorice powder
1 tsp aniseed extract

You'll also need
24 x 18cm baking tray
Temperature probe or
  sugar thermometer

Line the baking tray with non-stick baking paper.

Place the blackcurrants in a pan with the water and simmer for 5 minutes to make a purée. Tip the contents of the pan into a sieve set over a bowl. Use a ladle to press the juice through so that you are left with a smooth mixture.

Place the blackcurrant purée and all the other ingredients in a large saucepan set on a low heat and cook, stirring, until the sugar has dissolved and the butter has melted. Increase the heat to medium-high and allow the mixture to boil without stirring. As the caramel cooks, use a pastry brush dipped in water to wash down the insides of the pan to prevent any crystals forming.

As soon as the caramel has reached 121°C, immediately remove it from the heat and pour into the prepared tin. Prick out any air bubbles with the tip of a sharp knife and allow the mixture to cool fully in a dry place overnight. The next day, cut the caramel into small squares and wrap in pieces of non-stick baking paper.

Makes
64

PASSIONFRUIT CARAMELS

Sharply aromatic and sherbet-like, the flavour of passionfruit pierces the rich smooth flavours of the caramel, balancing it perfectly.

Time: 45 minutes plus
   overnight cooling

15–20 passionfruit
120ml double cream
200g unsalted butter
400g granulated sugar
200g demerara sugar

You'll also need
24 x 18cm baking tray
Temperature probe or sugar
   thermometer

Line the baking tray with non-stick baking paper.

Start by making passionfruit juice. Spoon out the pulp from the fruit into a small pan set over a medium heat and simmer for 5 minutes. Pour the passionfruit juice through a sieve into a bowl. Use a ladle to press the juice through. You should have 200ml passionfruit juice. If you are short of juice, simply top up with a little freshly squeezed orange juice.

Place the ingredients, including the passionfruit juice, in a large saucepan set on a low heat and cook. Stir until the sugar has dissolved and the butter has melted.

Increase the heat to medium-high and allow the mixture to boil without stirring.

As the caramel cooks, use a pastry brush dipped in water to wash down the insides of the pan to prevent any crystals forming.

As soon as the caramel has reached 121°C, immediately remove it from the heat and pour into the prepared tin. Prick out any air bubbles with the tip of a sharp knife and allow the mixture to cool fully in a dry place overnight. The next day, cut the caramel into small squares and wrap in pieces of non-stick baking paper.

Makes
48

SCOTTISH TABLET

Early recipes for tablet date from the 18th century and, although similar to fudge, tablet is more sugary and crystalline, and distinctly milky. Unlike fudge, tablet is beaten while hot, which causes the sugar to crystallise – be careful to beat it just enough to start the process off, otherwise you will end up with a hard lump of sugary mixture in the pan.

Time: 30 minutes plus 2
  hours to set
——

500g granulated sugar
100ml milk
50g salted butter, plus
  extra for greasing
200g sweetened
  condensed milk

You'll also need
16–20cm-square baking tin
Temperature probe or
  sugar thermometer
Vinyl or rubber gloves

Lightly grease the baking tin with butter.

Place the sugar and milk in a large pan and allow the sugar to start dissolving into the milk for 5 minutes. Transfer the pan to a low heat, add the butter and stir until the sugar is dissolved. Add the condensed milk and raise the heat to medium-high. Allow the mixture to boil, stirring occasionally. Use a pastry brush dipped in hot water to wash down the insides of the pan to prevent crystals forming too early in the process. Cook the mixture until it reaches 118°C, then remove from the heat and stand the pan on a heatproof surface.

Wearing gloves for safety, beat the tablet with the whisk until you can feel the mixture starting to form crystals – a process known as 'graining'. Stir until the mixture is evenly grained and pour quickly into the prepared tin. Spread the mixture out evenly and tap the tin gently on the work surface to release any bubbles.

When the mixture is nearly cold, score the surface with a sharp knife into 2–3cm pieces. Break into pieces once completely cool and store in an airtight container or tin.

Makes
100

VANILLA FUDGE

This is a very simple fudge recipe but excellent nonetheless. Evaporated milk is used here, which makes the fudge richer than those made with milk or cream.

Time: 1 hour plus
  overnight cooling

1kg granulated sugar
1 x 410g tin evaporated milk
125ml water
125g salted butter
Seeds from 2 vanilla pods

You'll also need
2 x 18cm-square baking tins
Temperature probe or sugar
  thermometer

Line the baking tins with non-stick baking paper.

Place all of the ingredients in a large pan set on a low heat. Stir until the sugar has dissolved and the butter has melted. Increase the heat to medium-high and bring the mixture to a boil.

When the mixture reaches 110°C, reduce the heat to medium and cook until the mixture reaches 117°C, stirring occasionally, and while it cooks wash down the insides of the pan with a pastry brush dipped in hot water. You will notice that the temperature increases very slowly at first, so be patient.

Fill your sink with an inch or two of cold water as you will need to cool the base of the pan.

Briefly dip the base of the pan in your water-filled sink to arrest the cooking process. Stand the pan on a heatproof surface and allow the fudge to cool to 50°C. Using a wooden spoon or a large whisk, beat the fudge until it thickens and holds its shape. Spread into the prepared tins and lay another sheet of non-stick baking paper on top and smooth it gently.

Allow the fudge to cool fully overnight before cutting into 1.5cm squares. Store in an airtight container or tin.

Makes
150

CHOCOLATE FUDGE

I like to use a really dark chocolate for this recipe – preferably one with at least 70% cocoa, which will stand up to the richness of the sweet buttery fudge.

Time: 1 hour plus overnight
  cooling
———
375g dark chocolate,
  chopped into small pieces
400g double cream
1kg granulated sugar
125ml water
125g salted butter

You'll also need
2 x 18cm-square baking tins
Temperature probe or
  sugar thermometer

Line the baking tins with non-stick baking paper.

Place all of the ingredients in a large pan set on a low heat. Stir until the sugar has dissolved and the butter has melted. Increase the heat to medium-high and bring the mixture to the boil. When the mixture reaches 110°C, reduce the heat to medium and cook until the mixture reaches 114°C, stirring occasionally, and while it cooks wash down the insides of the pan with a pastry brush dipped in hot water. You will notice that the temperature increases very slowly at first, so be patient.

Fill your sink with an inch or two of cold water as you will need to cool the base of the pan.

Briefly dip the base of the pan in your water-filled sink to arrest the cooking process. Stand the pan on a heatproof surface and allow the fudge to cool to 50°C. Using a wooden spoon or a large whisk, beat the fudge until it thickens and holds its shape. Spread into the prepared tins and lay over another sheet of non-stick baking paper on top and smooth the surface gently.

Allow the fudge to cool fully overnight before removing the covering paper and cutting into 1.5cm squares. Store in an airtight container or tin.

Makes
48

ORANGE FUDGE

With very few exceptions, we have access to all fruits on a year-round basis, unlike Isabella. In the winter months one seasonal treat is the Seville orange, so use these for this lovely recipe when you can get hold of them. Clementines and mandarins also give delicious results.

**Time: 1 hour plus overnight
  cooling**

500g granulated sugar
180ml single cream
2½ tbsp golden syrup
60g salted butter
Zest and juice of 1 orange,
  preferably Seville

You'll also need
18cm-square baking tin
Temperature probe or sugar
  thermometer

Line the baking tin with non-stick baking paper.

Place all the ingredients apart from the orange zest into a large pan set on a low heat. Stir until the sugar has dissolved and the butter has melted. Increase the heat to medium-high and bring the mixture to the boil.

When the mixture reaches 110°C, reduce the heat to medium and cook until the mixture reaches 116°C, stirring occasionally, and while it cooks wash down the insides of the pan with a pastry brush dipped in hot water. You will notice that the temperature increases very slowly at first, so be patient.

Fill your sink with an inch or two of cold water as you will need to cool the base of the pan.

Add the orange zest to the pan and briefly dip the base of the pan in your water-filled sink to arrest the cooking process. Stand the pan on a heatproof surface and allow the fudge to cool to 50°C. Using a wooden spoon or a large whisk, beat the fudge until it thickens and holds its shape. Spread into the prepared tin and lay a sheet of non-stick baking paper on top and smooth the surface gently.

Cool fully overnight before cutting into 1.5cm squares. Store in an airtight container or tin.

Makes
50–60

MAPLE PECAN FUDGE

An all-American recipe that is lighter than traditional fudge with the pleasing crunch of toasted pecan nuts.

Time: 1 hour plus overnight
to cool

120g pecan nuts
500g granulated sugar
125ml water
120ml pure maple syrup
130ml milk
2 tbsp golden syrup
25g salted butter

You'll also need
18cm-square baking
tray or tin
Temperature probe or
sugar thermometer

Preheat the oven to 150°C/300°F/Gas mark 2. Line the baking tray with non-stick baking paper. Fill your sink with an inch or two of cold water as you will need to cool the base of the pan.

Place the pecan nuts on a baking tray and toast the nuts for 20–25 minutes until they are a mid-brown colour inside – break a nut in half to check that they are cooked through otherwise they won't develop their full flavour. Transfer the nuts to a small bowl and allow them to cool, then break them into small pieces.

While the nuts are toasting, prepare the fudge base. Place the remaining ingredients into a large pan set on a low heat. Stir until the sugar has dissolved and the butter has melted. Increase the heat to medium and bring the mixture to the boil. When the mixture reaches 110°C, reduce the heat to medium and cook until the mixture reaches 116°C, stirring occasionally, and while it cooks wash down the insides of the pan with a pastry brush dipped in hot water. You will notice that the temperature increases very slowly at first, so be patient.

Briefly dip the base of the pan in your water-filled sink to arrest the cooking process. Stand the pan on a heatproof surface and allow the fudge to cool to 50°C. Using a wooden spoon or a large whisk, beat the fudge until it thickens and holds its shape. Spread into the prepared tin, scatter the pecans evenly over the surface then lay over a sheet of non-stick baking paper to smooth it gently.

Allow the fudge to cool fully overnight before cutting into 1.5cm squares. Store in an airtight tin or container.

Tip: Fudge made with milk occasionally splits when it is beaten. If you notice it becoming greasy, do not worry. Knead the fudge till it cools and the butter will easily be reabsorbed. You can then roll the fudge out into the tray.

Makes
48

HAZELNUT AND RAISIN FUDGE

Crunchy hazelnuts and chewy raisins add a wonderful texture to this lovely fudge. You can vary the type of nuts to suit your liking.

**Time: I hour 20 minutes
plus overnight cooling**

100g peeled hazelnuts
 (see page 124)
250g granulated sugar
250g demerara sugar
180ml single cream
2½ tbsp golden syrup
125ml water
60g salted butter
100g raisins

You'll also need
18cm-square baking tin
Temperature probe or
 sugar thermometer

Preheat the oven to 120°C/250°F/Gas mark ½. Line the baking tin with non-stick baking paper.

Place the hazelnuts on a small baking tray and bake for 40 minutes or so until they are a mid-brown colour inside – break a nut in half to check that they are cooked through otherwise they won't develop their full flavour.

Place the sugars, cream, golden syrup, water and butter in a large pan set on a low heat. Stir until the sugar has dissolved and the butter has melted. Increase the heat to medium-high and bring the mixture to the boil.

When it reaches 110°C, reduce the heat and cook until the mixture reaches 116°C, stirring occasionally, and while it cooks wash down the insides of the pan with a pastry brush dipped in hot water. You will notice that the temperature increases very slowly at first, so be patient. Fill your sink with an inch or two of cold water as you will need to cool the base of the pan.

Add the nuts and raisins to the pan and briefly dip the base of the pan in your water-filled sink to arrest the cooking process. Stand the pan on a heatproof surface and allow the fudge to cool to 50°C. Using a wooden spoon or a large whisk, beat the fudge until it thickens and holds its shape. Spread into the prepared tin then lay over a sheet of non-stick baking paper and smooth the surface gently.

Allow the fudge to cool fully overnight before cutting into 1.5cm squares. Store in an airtight container or tin.

Makes
48

COCONUT CARDAMOM FUDGE

This delicious dairy-free fudge is delightfully flavoured with citrusy cardamom and textured with fresh coconut strands. If you can't find fresh coconuts you can substitute desiccated coconut – use 180g, along with 250ml coconut water, which is available in most supermarkets and healthfood shops.

Time: 1 hour 20 minutes
  plus overnight to cool

2 fresh coconuts
10 cardamom pods, crushed
  lightly
120ml water
700g granulated sugar

You'll also need
18cm-square baking tin
30cm-square piece of
  muslin
Temperature probe or
  sugar thermometer

Line the baking tin with non-stick baking paper.

To extract the coconut water, have ready a small bowl. Stand a coconut so that the end with the three eyes points uppermost. Use a metal skewer or fine, clean, screwdriver to pierce the one soft eye. Tip the coconut upside down and shake to release the water inside. When you have extracted all of the water from two coconuts, strain it through a clean piece of muslin into a measuring jug. You will need 250ml for this recipe – any excess can be drunk or used in another recipe (it is delicious).

To extract the flesh from the coconut, wrap it in a clean cloth, and tap it sharply on the edge of a brick or stone to fracture the shell. Remove the coconut flesh and peel off the brown skin using a sharp knife or potato peeler. Grate the flesh and weigh 180g for this recipe.

Remove the small brown seeds from the cardamom pods and grind the seeds in a pestle and mortar.

Place all the ingredients (reserving a little of the grated coconut flesh) into a large pan set on a low heat. Stir until the sugar has dissolved. Increase the heat to medium-high and bring the mixture to the boil. When it reaches 110°C, reduce the heat to medium and cook until the mixture reaches 116°C, stirring occasionally, and while it cooks wash down the insides of the pan with a pastry brush dipped in hot water. You will notice that the temperature increases very slowly at first, so be patient.

Half-fill your sink with cold water as you will need to cool the base of the pan.

Briefly dip the base of the pan in your water-filled sink to arrest the cooking process. Stand the pan on a heatproof surface and allow the fudge to cool to 50°C. Using a wooden spoon, beat the fudge until it thickens and holds its shape. Spread into the prepared tin and smooth the surface by laying another sheet of non-stick baking paper on top and patting it gently.

Allow the fudge to cool fully overnight before removing the paper and cutting into 1.5cm squares and sprinkle with the reserved coconut flesh. Store in an airtight tin.

Makes
80

MUSCOVADO RUM FUDGE

The deep intense flavour of muscovado sugar harmonises perfectly with dark rum, while the spices add an exotic note.

Time: 1 hour plus
  overnight cooling

850g muscovado sugar
300ml double cream
125ml water
125g salted butter
100ml dark rum
Seeds from 1 vanilla pod
½ tsp ground cinnamon
Large pinch allspice
½ tsp ground nutmeg

You'll also need
24 x 18cm baking tray
Temperature probe or sugar
  thermometer

Line the baking tray with non-stick baking paper.

Place all of the ingredients in a large pan set on a low heat. Stir until the sugar has dissolved and the butter has melted. Increase the heat to medium-high and bring the mixture to the boil. When the mixture reaches 110°C, reduce the heat to medium and cook until the mixture reaches 116°C, stirring occasionally, and while it cooks wash down the insides of the pan with a pastry brush dipped in hot water. You will notice that the temperature increases very slowly at first, so be patient.

Fill your sink with an inch or two of cold water as you will need to cool the base of the pan.

Briefly dip the base of the pan in your water-filled sink to arrest the cooking process. Stand the pan on a heatproof surface and allow the fudge to cool to 50°C. Using a wooden spoon or a large whisk, beat the fudge until it thickens and holds its shape. Spread into the prepared tins and smooth the surface by laying another sheet of non-stick baking paper on top and patting it gently.

Allow the fudge to cool fully overnight before removing the covering paper and cutting into 1.5cm squares. Store in an airtight container or tin.

Makes
100

WHISKY HONEY FUDGE

In order to get a good clear whisky flavour, use a strongly flavoured smoky Isla malt which marries wonderfully with heather honey.

Time: 1 hour plus
overnight cooling

—

900g granulated sugar
100g heather honey – or
   your favourite honey
400ml double cream
125ml water
125g salted butter
100ml Islay malt whisky

You'll also need
2 x 18cm-square
   baking tins
Temperature probe or sugar
   thermometer

Line the baking tins with non-stick baking paper.

Place all of the ingredients in a large pan set on a low heat. Stir until the sugar has dissolved and the butter has melted. Increase the heat to medium-high and bring the mixture to the boil. When the mixture reaches 110°C, reduce the heat to medium and cook until the mixture reaches 117°C, stirring occasionally, and while it cooks wash down the insides of the pan with a pastry brush dipped in hot water. You will notice that the temperature increases very slowly at first, so be patient.

Fill your sink with an inch or two of cold water as you will need to cool the base of the pan.

Briefly dip the base of the pan in your water-filled sink to arrest the cooking process. Stand the pan on a heatproof surface and allow the fudge to cool to 50°C. Using a wooden spoon or a large whisk, beat the fudge until it thickens and holds its shape. Spread into the prepared tins and smooth the surface by laying another sheet of non-stick baking paper on top and patting it gently.

Allow the fudge to cool fully overnight before removing the covering paper and cutting into 1.5cm squares. Store in an airtight container or tin.

Note: Fudge made with cream occasionally splits when it is beaten. If you notice it becoming greasy, do not worry. Knead the fudge till it cools and the butter will easily be reabsorbed. You can then roll the fudge out into its tray.

Makes
60

CLOTTED CREAM AND BAILEY'S IRISH FUDGE

Rich and creamy in the extreme, this fudge is delicately flavoured with Bailey's Irish liqueur.

Time: I hour plus overnight
 cooling

500g granulated sugar
100g demerara sugar
240g clotted cream
125ml water
100ml Bailey's Irish liqueur
1 tbsp liquid glucose
30g unsalted butter

You'll also need
24 x 18cm baking tray
Temperature probe or
 sugar thermometer

Line the baking tray with non-stick baking paper.

Place all of the ingredients into a large pan set on a low heat. Stir until the sugar has dissolved and the butter has melted. Cook until the mixture reaches 116°C, stirring occasionally, and while it cooks wash down the insides of the pan with a pastry brush dipped in hot water. You will notice that the temperature increases very slowly at first, so be patient.

Fill your sink with an inch or two of cold water as you will need to cool the base of the pan.

Briefly dip the base of the pan in your water-filled sink to arrest the cooking process. Stand the pan on a heatproof surface and allow the fudge to cool to 50°C. Using a wooden spoon or a large whisk, beat the fudge until it thickens and holds its shape. Spread into the prepared tin and smooth the surface by laying another sheet of non-stick baking paper on top and patting it gently.

Allow the fudge to cool fully overnight before removing the covering paper and cutting into 1.5cm squares. Store in an airtight tin.

FRUIT

Fruit pastilles and candied fruits represent some of the oldest known sweets, and in fact are based on techniques similar to those used to preserve fruits for jams and jellies. Isabella Beeton gives many recipes for preserves, jellies and fruit pastes in her *Book of Household Management*, such was their importance to the Victorian cook.

Historically, fruits were not available year-round and so preserves and fruit sweets enabled the cook to 'store' fruits outside their traditional season. Fruits can be made into sweets using a variety of methods – be it fruit toffees, jellies, pastilles, leathers or jewel-like candied fruits.

Fresh fruit juices and pastes are some of our healthiest confections and have the advantage of being quick to make. Brief cooking at relatively low temperatures gives these sweets, above all others, clarity and freshness of flavour.

Wherever possible the natural flavour and colour of the original fruit is preserved, but this is not always possible. When mixtures using fruit are cooked to higher temperatures the ethereal flavour and aroma of the original fruit is lost.

The compounds that flavour fruits are not heat stable, meaning that temperatures above 130°C causes the flavours to break down and caramelise. Although you can use fruit juices to make sweets that are hard and brittle, they tend to lack their original freshness. To make hard and crisp fruit sweets such as lollies and lemon drops, natural extracts and oils are used to provide flavour, which can be jazzed up with the appropriate colours. You will find recipes for hard-boiled fruit sweets in chapter 1 (see page 24).

TIPS AND TECHNIQUES

GELATINE-SET SWEETS

Gelatine (see page 18) is often used to make rubbery fruit sweets that will not melt or be tacky. Because gelatine-set sweets are not cooked to a high temperature or high sugar concentration (which would help preserve them) they do not keep and are best kept chilled in the fridge and eaten within a week of making. Unless a recipe specifies otherwise, do not heat the gelatine above 40°C or it will not set properly.

Stripy jellies are great fun to make and, as they are barely heated, safe for children to make with supervision. Contrasting colours and flavours can be used to provide endless variety, and as they are made with fresh fruit juices, they are reasonably healthy, like the Striped Gummy Worms on page 102.

Gelatine is also sometimes used in making Turkish delight, a slow-cooked confection that I like to make using real fruit juices. Although not strictly authentic, recipes that use gelatine are quicker to make and, because they are not cooked for an extended period, the freshness of the fruit flavour is not lost as it sometimes is in traditional recipes.

FRUIT LEATHERS

These are a healthy kind of sweet or chew that can be made without sugar. Fruit purées are simply spread in thin layers before being dried in a low oven or dehydrator for several hours until firm enough to peel off their backing paper and store more or less indefinitely. They are useful if you are faced with a glut of fruit and want to preserve it, but are relatively time consuming.

Dehydrators are widely available from national kitchenware stockists (see page 202). They are small kitchen appliances that are the size of a kitchen steamer and are easy to use. Care needs to be taken to ensure good airflow throughout the dehydrator and that the machine is not left unattended as they can get rather hot. The actual time it takes to make a leather depends both on the water content of the original purée and the relative humidity – in wet weather expect them to take longer to dry than on a fresh dry day.

DRIED FRUIT PASTES

A wonderful variety of dried fruit is available to us today, often plump and ready to eat. The texture of apricots, dates and prunes is luxurious and mimics the feel of richer, dairy ingredients in the mouth. Pastes made using dried fruits are delicious in their own right and not solely as a replacement for more calorific sweets. Spices can be added, alcohol too, as in the case of the Dried Fig 'Salami' on page 109, which is absolutely delicious.

CANDIED FRUITS

Candying represents one of the oldest preserving techniques, and we commonly use both candied peel and glacé cherries in everyday baking.

Essentially, the water content of the fruit is replaced by sugar syrup that is incrementally strengthened over a period of 8–10 days. Apart from the preparation time, there is little complicated work involved. The end product is a crystalline and very sweet product that, if made properly, will keep indefinitely.

Fruits that are very soft or have a very thin skin are not easily candied as they tend to break up during the process.

Fruits to use for candying

* Pineapple
* Small citrus fruits/slices of fruit or fruit peel
* Cherries
* Mango slices

Fruits to avoid

* Berries
* Large stone fruit such as plums and peaches

Fresh ginger root is another classic contender for candying and the method for this can be found on page 156 where it is also dipped in chocolate.

FRUIT PASTILLES

Sparkling pastilles brimming with fresh fruit flavours are easy and quick to make. The key to successful production is pectin powder (see page 18) which is available from stockists listed at the back of the book. Pectin powder will clump together if added straight to liquid, so it is essential to mix it first with dry sugar before adding to the mixture.

Clear, distinct flavours work best when making fruit pastilles: apricot, passionfruit, blackcurrant, raspberry and rhubarb all give good results. To make a soft purée of any hard fruit, as a rule you should first simmer the fruit with half its weight of clear apple juice until it is soft enough to sieve. The apple juice works well as a background flavour without dominating. When using passionfruit, you need only sieve the seeds from the pulp. In the case of soft berries that are usually eaten raw, a clear fresh juice can be made by dripping crushed fruit through a piece of muslin overnight (see Strawberry Pastilles, page 116).

Cooking pastilles

Once you have your fruit purée, cooking the pastilles is quick and straightforward. The ingredients are first stirred over a low heat to dissolve the sugar before boiling the mixture to 108–109°C, by which time it will be jam-like and thickened. The mixture can then be set in a cling-film lined tray and allowed to cool until firm enough to cut into lozenge shapes.

Makes
400g

FROSTED REDCURRANTS

Isabella used a mixture of fruits frosted in sugar for a summer dessert. Choose large bunches of currants and prepare these a day or two before you need them to allow the sugar time to dry. They can be eaten as a treat, or used to decorate a cake.

Time: 30 minutes plus
  overnight drying time

200g redcurrants, stems
  attached
1 egg white
2 tsp water
200g caster sugar

Line a large baking tray with non-stick baking paper.

Wash the bunches of currants in cold water and allow them to dry on a clean towel.

Beat the egg white and water together with a fork until the mixture is frothy. Dip each bunch of currants into the egg white mixture, allow any excess to drip off, then toss the currants into the sugar. Lay the frosted currants out onto the prepared tray and allow them to dry in a warm, dry place overnight. The frosted currants should be stored in the fridge in an airtight tin – they will keep for up to a week. Alternatively, you can keep the redcurrants in the freezer once they are dried and use them throughout the year.

Makes
60

LEMON TURKISH DELIGHT

The texture of Turkish delight is carefully controlled to give a yielding but not rubbery texture, so that the exquisite citrus flavour comes to the fore. If you can find Meyer lemons, which appear on the market in the early summer, use them as their sherbet flavour is rare and unique.

Time: 1 hour

15 lemons
30g gelatine leaves
500g granulated sugar
30g cornflour
2 tbsp icing sugar mixed
  with 1 tbsp cornflour, for
  dusting

You'll also need
60cm-square piece muslin
  or cheesecloth
20cm-square baking tray

Preheat the oven to 140°C/275°C/Gas mark 1. Line the baking tray with non-stick baking paper.

Zest four of the lemons and set aside. Cut all the lemons in half and squeeze the juice through a fine sieve into a small bowl.

Measure the juice – you should have at least 300–350ml. If you do not, top up the quantity with clear apple juice so that you have 300ml. If you have spare juice, keep it and drink it mixed with sparkling mineral water and a touch of sugar. You are now ready to move on to the next stage of the recipe.

Immerse the gelatine leaves in a bowl of cold water to soften them. Mix the juice, sugar and zest in a large saucepan set on a medium heat. Stir to dissolve the sugar, then increase the heat and boil for 1 minute. Slake the cornflour with a little water and add this to the mixture along with the gelatine, squeezed to remove any excess water. Reduce the heat and cook, stirring, for 6 minutes until the mixture has thickened. Remove from the heat.

Pour the mixture into the prepared tin and allow to set overnight covered with a layer of cling film. When the Turkish delight has set, use a sharp knife dipped in hot water to cut the mixture into small squares approximately 1.5cm across. Toss the cubes in a mixture of icing sugar and cornflour.

Makes
60

RHUBARB AND ROSE TURKISH DELIGHT

This Turkish delight recipe uses gelatine to help achieve a firm texture, which is not entirely traditional but does minimise the otherwise lengthy cooking of the confection.

Time: I hour

400g rhubarb – use the
  pinkest you can find
200ml clear apple juice
30g gelatine leaves
500g granulated sugar
½ tsp citric acid (optional)
30g cornflour
¼ tsp rose extract
2 tbsp icing sugar mixed
  with I tbsp cornflour, for
  dusting

You'll also need
60cm-square piece muslin
  or cheesecloth
20cm-square baking tray

Preheat the oven to 140°C/275°C/Gas mark I. Line the baking tray with non-stick baking paper.

Wash the rhubarb and cut it into 1–2cm lengths. Place in a ceramic baking dish. Bring the apple juice to a boil in a small saucepan, and pour over the rhubarb. Lay a sheet of non-stick baking paper over the surface and place the dish in the oven for 40 minutes or until the rhubarb is very soft.

Set a colander over a large bowl and line with muslin. Tip in the rhubarb mixture and allow the juices to collect in the bowl for approximately 4 hours or overnight, covered in a sheet of cling film.

Measure the juice – you should have at least 300–350ml. If you do not, top up with clear apple juice to get 300ml. If you have spare juice, keep it and drink it mixed with sparkling mineral water and a touch of sugar.

Immerse the gelatine leaves in a bowl of cold water to soften them. Mix the rhubarb juice, sugar and citric acid, if using, in a large saucepan set on a medium heat. Stir to dissolve the sugar, then increase the heat and boil for I minute. Slake the cornflour with a little water and add this to the mixture along with the gelatine, squeezed to remove any excess water. Reduce the heat and cook, stirring, for 6 minutes until the mixture has thickened. Add the rose extract and remove from the heat.

Pour the mixture into the prepared tin and allow to set overnight covered with a layer of cling film. When the Turkish delight has set, use a sharp knife dipped in hot water to cut the mixture into small squares approximately 1.5cm across. Toss the cubes in a mixture of icing sugar and cornflour.

Tip: A small amount of citric acid can be used to sharpen the flavour if you like.

Makes
60

STRIPED GUMMY WORMS

Gummy worms are set using gelatine and so do not keep for more than a few days. They are great fun to make for children's parties and use real fruit juice for a better flavour.

Time: 30 minutes plus 1
 hour setting time

30 gelatine leaves
150ml clear apple juice
150ml blood orange juice
180g granulated sugar
300g liquid glucose
½ tsp lavender extract
Blue and red food colouring
 (paste is best)
Sunflower or almond oil, for
 greasing

You'll also need
Deep baking tin, roughly
 24 x 18cm

Sprinkle a little water on the baking tin and line with cling film. Dab a little sunflower oil onto a piece of kitchen paper and use this to grease the cling film lightly and evenly.

Divide the gelatine leaves into two equal portions and place each portion in a separate bowl of cold water to soften.

Place the two juices in two separate pans and add 90g sugar and 150g liquid glucose to each. Add the lavender extract to the apple juice pan, along with a tiny amount of blue and red food colouring, if desired, to make a deep purple colour.

Warm the apple juice over a low heat, stirring to dissolve the sugar and glucose – there is no need to bring it to the boil. When the sugar has dissolved and the mixture is hot, remove one portion of gelatine from its water, squeeze out any excess water, and add it to the hot juice. Stir to dissolve the gelatine and pour the mixture through a sieve into the prepared tin. Set aside for 30 minutes to cool.

While the purple layer sets, warm the orange juice over a low heat, stirring to dissolve the sugar and glucose – there is no need to bring it to the boil. When the sugar has dissolved and the mixture is hot, remove the second portion of gelatine, squeeze out any excess water, and add it to the hot juice. Stir to dissolve the gelatine and pour the mixture through a sieve into a clean bowl. Allow the orange jelly to cool fully, before pouring over the set purple jelly. Cool the two-tone jelly for another 30 minutes or so until it is set.

When the jelly is completely set, turn the mixture out onto a lightly oiled piece of cling film set on a cutting board. Use a knife dipped in hot water to cut the sheet of jelly in half lengthways, and then cut each half into thin strips, making your worms. Store in an airtight container in the fridge for up to a week.

Makes
150g

SPICED PLUM LEATHER

Either use an oven set to its lowest heat or a dehydrator to make these healthy sweet treats. As the plum paste dries out, the flavour concentrates and sweetens a little. If you like, you can add a little sugar, but I think the recipe is just fine without.

Time: 30 minutes plus 8–12
  hours drying time

1kg ripe purple plums
100ml cloudy apple juice
1 tsp ground cinnamon
200g granulated sugar
  (optional)

You'll also need
Dehydrator (optional)

If using a dehydrator, line it with rings of non-stick baking paper. If using an oven, turn it on to its lowest setting and line three large baking trays with non-stick baking paper.

Wash the plums and cut them into small pieces, discarding the stones. Place the fruit in a large pan with the apple juice and set it on a medium heat. Cook, stirring, until the plums are completely reduced. Either sieve or liquidise the plums to make a thick purée. Add the cinnamon and sugar to taste – about 200g will make it sweet enough, but if you would like to keep the mixture healthy, you do not need to add any at all.

Stir until the sugar is completely dissolved, then spread the purée onto sheets of non-stick baking paper cut to fit your dehydrator or baking trays. Make sure that the purée is spread evenly, approximately 2–3mm thick.

If you are using a dehydrator, make sure you follow the manufacturer's instructions. Let the dehydrator run until the sheets of leather can be rolled off the paper and are no longer sticky. You will find that you may have to move the layers of purée from the top to the bottom of the dehydrator once or twice to ensure even drying.

For oven drying, preheat your oven to 80°C/200°F/¼ gas. Cook for 3–4 hours, then switch the oven off and leave to dry overnight. If you are using your oven the amount of purée you can dry at any time depends on how many shelves you have. You may find that you have to reserve some of the purée in the fridge to finish the leather the following day.

Tip: In very humid or wet weather the sheets will take longer to dry out. It is perfectly fine to let them dry for a few hours and then finish the following day. It is safer not to leave a dehydrator or oven switched on for several hours unattended.

Makes
100g

MANGO, LIME AND CARDAMOM LEATHER

A really exotic fruit leather that is surprisingly easy to make. Choose the most aromatic mangoes you can for this – Alphonso or Keitt are ideal because they have a lovely flavour and are less fibrous than other varieties.

Time: 30 minutes plus overnight to dry

800g ripe mangoes (about 2 medium fruit)
Juice of 2 limes
2 tsp cardamom pods

You'll also need
Dehydrator (optional)

If using a dehydrator, line it with rings of non-stick baking paper. If using an oven, turn it on to its lowest setting and line three large baking trays with non-stick baking paper.

Peel the mangoes and cut the flesh into a bowl or the jug of a liquidiser. Add the lime juice.

Peel the cardamom pods and grind the brown seeds in a pestle and mortar or crush with the base of a heavy pan. Add the crushed seeds to the liquidiser. Purée the pulp and sieve if necessary. Spread the purée onto sheets of non-stick baking paper cut to fit your dehydrator or baking sheets. Make sure that the purée is spread evenly, approximately 2–3mm thick. If you are using a dehydrator, make sure you follow the manufacturer's instructions. Let the dehydrator run until the sheets of leather can be rolled off the paper and are no longer sticky. You will find that you may have to move the layers of purée from the top to the bottom of the dehydrator once or twice to ensure even drying. The process may take longer in humid weather (see Tip on page 103).

For oven drying, preheat your oven to 80°C/200°F/¼ gas. Cook for 3–4 hours, then switch the oven off and leave to dry overnight. If you are using your oven, the amount of purée you can dry at any time depends on how many shelves you have. You may find that you have to reserve some of the purée in the fridge to finish the leather the following day.

Makes
40–50

CARROT AND CLEMENTINE BALLS

Isabella wrote what may seem to us today an unusual recipe for carrot jam. In fact, carrots appear in confections around the world, and pair naturally with citrus flavours in particular.

Time: 1 hour plus overnight
  to dry

750g young carrots (peeled
  weight)
375g granulated sugar, plus
  100g for rolling
180ml clementine juice –
  from about 8 fruits

Cook the carrots in a steamer until they are very tender – this will take about 25 minutes. Lay them on clean tea towels to dry for several hours or overnight.

Purée the carrots in a food processor and sieve into a large pan, adding 375g granulated sugar and the clementine juice. Stir the mixture over a low heat until the sugar has dissolved and then increase the heat to medium. Stir constantly until the mixture has thickened to a paste – about 35–40 minutes. Remove the pan from the heat and allow the mixture to cool fully before rolling into balls approximately 2cm in diameter. Roll the balls in the remaining sugar and allow them to dry overnight on a tray lined with non-stick baking paper and covered lightly with cling film.

Store in a cool place and eat within a week.

DRIED FRUIT 'FUDGE'

Isabella writes that 'an inferior kind of date has lately become common, which are dried and have little flavour.' When buying dates, look for ones that are large, soft yet still firm, slightly wrinkled with a reddish-yellow colour on the outside.

Time: 25 minutes plus
  overnight to dry

—

125g flaked almonds
300g dried stoned prunes
300g dried apricots
300g stoned dates
  (preferably medjool)
45g honey

Lightly toast the almonds in a dry frying pan or a low oven for 5–10 minutes.

Mix the dried fruits in the bowl of a food processor and process until they are evenly smooth, adding the honey to soften the mixture. If it is very dry and stiff, you can add a little water or fruit juice to make it easier to blend, being careful not to add so much that the mixture will be too soft to roll into balls.

Form the mixture into even-sized balls roughly 2cm in diameter and roll each ball in the flaked almonds. Allow the balls to dry overnight on a clean tray lined with non-stick baking paper and covered lightly in cling film. Store in an airtight container or tin and eat within 2 weeks.

Makes
8

DRIED FIG 'SALAMI'

The best dried figs are to be found in the run-up to Christmas, wrapped in a ball of fig leaves. The leaves lend a coconut scent to the figs and makes them especially wonderful. If you cannot find these, use the best dried figs that you can.

The salami keeps indefinitely, and is best left to mature for a month, so if you are intending to make it as a gift for Christmas, allow yourself plenty of time. Serve with cheese or as a snack.

Time: 1 hour plus 1 month
  to mature

1kg dried figs
100g whole blanched
  almonds, roughly chopped
100g hazelnuts,
  roughly chopped
100g candied orange
  or grapefruit peel
  (see page 113)
200g dates, stoned,
  (preferably medjool)
  roughly chopped
100g unsalted pistachio nuts,
  roughly chopped
100g best-quality chocolate,
  coarsely grated
100ml brandy
1 tbsp fennel
  seeds (optional)
4 sheets 20 x 30cm edible
  wafer or rice paper,
  cut in half
Icing sugar, for dusting

Place all the ingredients in the bowl of a food processor and pulse the mixture until it is smooth and even.

Lightly dust a clean work surface with icing sugar and turn the mixture out onto it. Divide the mass in half three times, giving you 8 more or less even balls. Roll each ball out in a little icing sugar to a cylinder 3cm in diameter and then roll each one in a piece of wafer paper. Finally, wrap each salami in a piece of non-stick baking paper and store in a cool dry place to mature for a month. When they are ready, store in an airtight container or tin until needed.

Makes
500g

CANDIED PINEAPPLE

Isabella clearly thought highly of the pineapple as she gives three different recipes for candied pineapple. It is one of the best fruits to candy as its firm texture and clear flavour are not lost in the process. Don't be put off by the time it takes to make this recipe because you only spend a few minutes a day doing each phase – and trust me, the end result is well worth it.

Time: a few minutes a day
    for 14 days

——

2 medium pineapples
    (about 800g each)
About 1.5kg granulated
    sugar

You'll also need
Stainless steel or plastic
    cooling rack set over a
    large tray

Remove the stalk from the pineapple and trim off all of the skin neatly using a sharp or serrated knife. Also cut out the 'eyes' to make a neat, clean barrel of fruit. Slice the pineapples into 1.5cm-thick slices (or chunks) and remove the core using an apple corer or small pastry cutter. Weigh the prepared fruit and place it in a large stainless-steel pan. For every 500g fruit add 280ml water. Place the pan on a medium heat and simmer the pineapple slices until they are tender – this will take about 15 minutes. Turn the slices over from time to time so that they cook evenly.

Drain the slices, reserving the liquid. For every 280ml liquid, weigh 175g sugar and dissolve this over a medium heat. Place the fruit in layers in a deep ceramic or plastic tray and cover it with the hot syrup. On the second day, drain the fruit on a wire rack set over a tray and measure the syrup. For every 280g, add 55g sugar and dissolve this in a pan over a medium heat. Return the fruit to the ceramic tray and pour over the hot syrup.

On days 3, 4, 5, 6 and 7 repeat this second step.

On day 8, add 80g sugar for every 280ml syrup, boil to dissolve and pour over the fruit. Cover with cling film, place the fruit in a cool room and allow it to sit for a couple of days. On day 10, add 80g sugar to the syrup for each 280ml and once again pour it over the fruit. The syrup will by now be very crystalline. After four days, drain the fruit on a wire rack set on a tray. Leave the fruit in a warm dry room for a few hours to dry it out. Store in an airtight container in a cool place for up to a month.

BRAMBLE AND APPLE CANDIES

Purple hued and free to pick in the wild, brambles, or blackberries as they are also known, were oddly ignored by Isabella but work really well when used in combination with apples in this simple recipe.

Time: 1 hour

450g blackberries
½ cooking apple (100g),
  peeled, cored and
  chopped small
500g granulated sugar
½ tsp cream of tartar
180ml water

You'll also need
Temperature probe or sugar
  thermometer
20cm-square baking tin

Line the baking tin with non-stick baking paper.

Place the blackberries in the jug of a liquidiser and add the apple. Blend until smooth, adding a little water if necessary, then pass this mixture through a sieve into a large pan. Place the pan on a medium heat and bring to a simmer, stirring. Cook until the mixture is thickened to that of a thick conserve or jam.

Keep the mixture warm over a very low heat while you prepare a sugar syrup.

Place the sugar, cream of tartar and water in a medium pan over a low heat and cook, stirring until the sugar has all dissolved. Turn the heat to high and cook the syrup until it reaches 149°C. Immediately stir in the warm purée and stir to combine. Cook on a low to medium heat, stirring constantly until the mixture begins to look cloudy and thick, then pour into the prepared tin.

Allow the mixture to cool until it is firm enough to mark into even squares, then leave to cool completely. Unmould the sweets, separate them and layer between pieces of non-stick baking paper in an airtight container or tin.

Makes
800g

CANDIED PEEL

In the Book of Household Management, *Isabella notes that oranges are at their best and plentiful in the winter months, which remains the case. Slivers of candied peel can also be dipped in dark chocolate as an after-dinner treat.*

Time: 20 minutes plus 5 hours cooking over 3 days and 2 days drying

—

5 large naval oranges or pink grapefruit with thick peel
1.5–2kg granulated sugar

You'll also need
Stainless steel or plastic cooling rack set over a large tray

Make two cuts around each orange, so that you can peel off the skin in four equal segments, leaving the fruit intact (you can eat this later). Place the peel in a large stainless-steel pan. Cover with cold water, bring to the boil, and then discard the liquid. Repeat this process twice more, draining the peel after the third blanching. You will end up with about 650g peel, depending on the size of the fruit.

Make a syrup by dissolving 1kg sugar in 1 litre water in a large pan. Add the peel, return to the heat and simmer gently for about 2 hours, or until the peel is translucent and very tender. Remove the pan from the heat and leave to cool overnight.

The next day, remove the peel and boil the syrup again, then pour back over the peel and then leave overnight to cool.

On the third day, strain the syrup into a bowl and measure it – for every litre, add 1kg sugar. Place this in a pan over a medium heat and boil to dissolve the sugar. Pour back over the peel and again leave overnight to cool. Drain the pieces of peel on a wire rack set over a large tray to catch the syrup as it drips. Allow the peel to dry for 2 days in a warm, dry room until it begins to crystallise and feels dry to the touch. Once dry, pack the peel into freezer boxes and store until required.

Makes
16–20

CANDIED ORANGE SLICES

This recipe is based on Isabella's iced oranges, which she dries in front of a fire until they develop a fine white crystal layer. This method for making candied orange works well in a modern kitchen. For a special present, you can decorate the slices with edible silver leaf (see the recipe on page 158).

Time: 2 hours plus additional time for drying

2 oranges with thin skin (preferably Valencias)
250ml water
400g granulated sugar

Scrub the oranges in hot water to remove as much of the wax as possible.

Slice into 5mm-thin slices.

To cook the slices, it is easiest to use a very clean, shallow frying pan or sauté pan.

Place the water and sugar in the pan and bring the mixture to a simmer over a medium to high heat. Add the orange slices in layers and cook very slowly until the syrup is much reduced and the slices are translucent and just beginning to crystallise.

Transfer the slices to a wire rack set over a tray and allow them to cool and dry. If the weather is humid, you might find this is easier done in a very low oven.

When cool and dry, store between sheets of non-stick baking paper in an airtight tin. Store the leftover syrup in the fridge – it makes an excellent addition to cakes and flapjacks or can be added to cooked fruit compotes.

Makes
60

STRAWBERRY PASTILLES

These make a lovely mid-summer treat. Make this recipe only when the strawberries are in their full season, ripened with warm sunshine for the best flavour. Try to plan ahead because the pastilles take a couple of days to make.

Time: 45 minutes plus time
   to set

1kg strawberries, hulled
350g granulated sugar
10g pectin powder
100g liquid glucose
1 tbsp lemon juice
100g caster sugar, to finish

You'll also need
24 x 18cm baking tray
60cm-square piece muslin or
   cheesecloth
Temperature probe or sugar
   thermometer

Line the baking tray with non-stick baking paper.

Wash the strawberries and allow them to dry on a clean tea towel. Place the berries in a large bowl with 1 tablespoon of the sugar. Crush the berries, using a fork, just until they begin to release their juices. Tip them into a colander lined with muslin set over a large bowl. Place a sheet of cling film over the top and allow the juice to drain overnight in a cool place.

Measure the juice – you should have at least 500ml. If you do not, top up the quantity with clear apple juice. If you have spare juice, keep it and drink it mixed with sparkling mineral water with a touch of sugar. You are now ready to move on to the next stage of the recipe.

Mix together the pectin powder and sugar in a small bowl. Warm the strawberry juice and liquid glucose in a medium to large pan set on a low heat. Add the sugar and pectin mixture to the pan and stir to dissolve the sugar. When it has fully dissolved, raise the heat to high and boil the mixture until it reaches 108°C. Stir in the lemon juice.

Pour the mixture into the prepared baking tray and allow the mixture to set and fully cool – this will take a couple of hours. When you are ready to cut up the pastilles, turn the mixture out onto a clean cutting board that is sprinkled with caster sugar. Use a sharp knife to cut the jelly into squares or lozenges. Store in an airtight container or tin between layers of non-stick baking paper.

Makes
60

SPICED APPLE AND CINNAMON PASTILLES

A recipe for autumn days when apples are in good supply and local producers will have plenty of variety for you to choose from. Try a sharply flavoured apple juice to balance the sweetness of the recipe. I recommend cloudy apple juice because it usually has the best flavour.

Time: 45 minutes plus time
  to set

10g pectin powder
350g granulated sugar
500ml cloudy apple juice
100g liquid glucose
½ tsp ground cinnamon
1 tbsp lemon juice
100g caster sugar, for
  dusting

You'll also need
24 x 18cm baking tray
Temperature probe or sugar
  thermometer

Line the baking tray with non-stick baking paper.

Mix the pectin powder and sugar together in a small bowl. Warm the apple juice, liquid glucose and cinnamon in a medium pan set on a low heat. Add the sugar and pectin mixture to the pan and stir to dissolve the sugar. When the sugar has fully dissolved, raise the heat to high and boil the mixture until it reaches 108°C. Stir in the lemon juice.

Pour the mixture into the prepared baking tray and allow the mixture to set and fully cool. When you are ready to cut up the pastilles, turn the mixture out onto a clean cutting board that is sprinkled with caster sugar. Use a sharp knife to cut the jelly into squares or lozenges. Store in an airtight container or tin between layers of non-stick baking paper.

Makes
60

RHUBARB AND ELDERFLOWER PASTILLES

Pale pink and sherbet-like, these fabulous jellies are well worth making. Choose the pinkest rhubarb you can find to achieve the best result. Elderflowers are available in hedgerows in the early summer, but you can always use elderflower cordial if you cannot find any fresh flowers. You'll need to plan ahead because the pastilles take two days to make.

Time: 45 minutes plus time
   to set

500g pink rhubarb
300ml clear apple juice
2 heads elderflower or
   2 tbsp elderflower cordial
10g pectin powder
350g granulated sugar
100g liquid glucose
1 tbsp lemon juice
100g caster sugar, for dusting

You'll also need
24 x 18cm baking tray
60cm-square piece muslin or
   cheesecloth
Temperature probe or sugar
   thermometer

Preheat the oven to 140°C/275°F/Gas mark 1. Line the baking tray with non-stick baking paper.

Wash the rhubarb and cut it into 1–2cm lengths. Place in a ceramic baking dish. Bring the apple juice to the boil in a small pan, and pour over the rhubarb. Add the elderflowers or cordial to the dish, pushing the flowers under the surface. Lay a sheet of non-stick baking paper over the surface and place the dish in the oven for 40 minutes or until the rhubarb is very soft.

Set a colander over a large bowl and line with muslin. Tip in the rhubarb mixture and allow the juices to collect in the bowl for about 4 hours or preferably overnight, covered in a sheet of cling film.

Measure the juice – you should have at least 500ml. If you do not, top up the quantity with clear apple juice. If you have spare juice, keep it and drink it mixed with sparkling mineral water and a touch of sugar. You are now ready to move on to the next stage of the recipe.

Mix together the pectin powder and sugar in a small bowl. Warm the juice and liquid glucose in a medium to large pan set on a low heat. Add the sugar and pectin mixture to the pan and stir to dissolve the sugar. When it has fully dissolved, raise the heat to high and boil the mixture until it reaches 108°C. Stir in the lemon juice.

Pour the mixture into the prepared baking tray and allow the mixture to set and fully cool – this will take a couple of hours. When you are ready to cut up the pastilles, turn the mixture out onto a clean cutting board sprinkled with caster sugar. Use a sharp knife to cut the jelly into squares or lozenges. Store in an airtight container or tin between layers of non-stick baking paper.

NUTS

Isabella rightly pointed out in her *Book of Household Management* that nuts are a seasonal and special treat; something we are less aware of today as we can buy packets of nuts year-round. By early September, the first of the cobnuts and filberts find their way into the markets, green and still wrapped in their papery sheaths. These are nuts for eating while still 'wet' and fresh and are best on their own. In Isabella's day, fresh nuts were served as part of a grand dessert, piled with their leaves alongside tempting bowls of fruit and fancy boxes of chocolate displayed to demonstrate the wealth and abundance of the autumn harvest.

Later in the autumn, ripe nuts appear in the shops, brown now and intact in their shells. These nuts are likely to be the tastiest, fattest and most suitable for sweet making because they will have the best flavour. At other times of year, it is advisable to avoid buying nuts in their shells as you may find dehydrated kernels inside which will be musty and unusable. Isabella warns against buying nuts beyond the end of winter, imploring her readers to check against the rancidity of walnuts and their oil. Look at the nuts in the packet – if they appear shrivelled or dry, reject them and buy plump, fresh looking nuts in preference.

The many delicious types of nuts available have among the highest food values of any natural product, being rich in oils and minerals. They are versatile ingredients for baker and confectioner alike. Whether pounded into fine marzipan, flaked as a coating, roasted for intensity or enrobed in chocolate, they add an alluring richness to sugary mixtures. Nuts appear frequently in continental confections, often being roasted and pounded with dark chocolate and cream to create sensational pralines.

TIPS AND TECHNIQUES

STORING NUTS

Because of their fat content, it is a good idea to store nuts in a cool place, or in a sealed container in the fridge. If stored in a hot or humid place, the oils will more readily oxidise and go rancid in which case they will spoil your recipe.

SHELLING

Metal nut crackers are common, but must be used carefully as they are likely to crush the shell and the soft kernel inside. Alternatively, use a small hammer to gently tap the shell, peeling it off carefully – tap too hard though and you will damage the kernel.

PEELING AND BLANCHING NUTS

It is possible to buy nuts ready peeled, which is an advantage for the busy cook. If you only have nuts with their skins intact, however, it is perfectly possible to peel them at home.

Almonds and pistachios – are best peeled by blanching them in boiling water. To do this, pour boiling water over the nuts, and leave them for 1–2 minutes. Carefully remove a couple of nuts at a time using a small fork, and use your fingers to peel off the skin. Spread the peeled nuts out on a clean tea towel to dry before using.

Walnuts and pecans – although not usually peeled, these can be blanched, but their skins are tougher to remove. Use a small knife to pare away the skin in small portions. This is very time consuming, but results in a delicious nut without the tannic flavour of the skin.

Hazelnuts – are best peeled by roasting them gently on a tray in a low oven for 20–30 minutes until they have a rich dark colour. The peel gradually dries and can be removed once the nuts are toasted by rubbing the hot nuts in a clean tea towel. Any persistent pieces of skin can be pared away using a small knife.

Chestnuts – are most easily peeled when very hot but while the kernels inside are still raw and hard. The inner skin can sometimes be very stubborn to remove, especially if the kernel inside is fully cooked and therefore soft. Using a sharp knife, cut a small flap at the base of each nut – approximately 5mm long, which will allow the heat and water to penetrate without splitting the nut. Boil a few chestnuts at a time for 5 minutes or so, and peel them while still hot. Don a pair of vinyl gloves to peel the nuts, as the fibrous skin can irritate if trapped under your finger. The chestnuts can then be poached in hot water or steamed to cook until soft.

ROASTING OR TOASTING NUTS

Some recipes for nutty sweets require you to roast or toast the nut kernels to intensify the flavour. This is best done at a relatively low temperature so that the nut toasts through to the centre evenly rather than purely on the surface. Spread the nuts out evenly on a baking tray in a thin layer and roast in a low oven (between 140–160°C)until they are an even mid-brown all over. The nuts should then be allowed to cool. As they do so they will crisp up. Store cooked nuts in a sealed container when fully cold.

CHOPPING NUTS

This is best done in a food processor, pulsing the nuts until the mixture is evenly chopped to the degree you require. Take care not to leave the machine running or the nuts may well be reduced into an oily paste. Alternatively, you can use a sharp knife to chop them on a clean cutting board.

GRINDING NUTS

When making truffle fillings using pistachios or roasted hazelnuts, you may be required to grind the nuts to a fine paste until they just begin to release their oils. This can be done either in a food processor or pestle and mortar. Simply grind the nuts to an even paste ensuring that no chunks remain before amalgamating them with the rest of your ingredients.

Makes
45–50

COCONUT AND RASPBERRY ICE

A simple confection to make with children – no cooking involved but delicious and a good keeper – although it is unlikely to last for long! If you would like to make the recipe more sophisticated, you can half-dip the pieces in melted dark or milk chocolate.

Time: 45 minutes plus 2–3
  hours drying time

340g icing sugar
300g desiccated coconut
397g tin sweetened
  condensed milk
¼ tsp red food colouring
1 tsp raspberry extract
  (optional)

Sieve the icing sugar into a large bowl, stir in the desiccated coconut and finally knead in the condensed milk. Halve the mass and to one half add the red colouring and raspberry extract, if desired. Knead this thoroughly through the mixture.

Lay a piece of non-stick baking paper on your work surface and spread the white half of the mixture into a 5–8mm thick rectangle. Do the same to the pink mixture and lay it on top, so that you have paper both on the top and the bottom of the mixture. Using a rolling pin, flatten the mixture to the thickness you desire.

Cut the coconut ice into 2cm cubes and place these on a tray lined with paper to dry for a couple of hours. Store in an airtight tin – it will keep for up to a week.

Makes
25–30

STUFFED MEDJOOL DATES

Medjool dates are at their best in the winter months – as Isabella says in her Book of Household Management, *choose plump dates that are not wrinkled.*

Time: 45 minutes

50g flaked almonds
500g best-quality medjool
  dates
125g icing sugar
125g ground almonds
1 tsp egg yolk
1 tbsp orange liqueur

Toast the flaked almonds by placing them in a dry frying pan over a low to medium heat and tossing them until they are lightly golden brown.

Remove the stones from the dates by cutting a slit along the surface of each one. Work carefully so as not to spoil the appearance of the skin. Discard the stones. Make the marzipan by mixing together the icing sugar and almonds in a medium bowl then adding the yolk and enough liqueur to make a smooth soft dough.

Using your fingers, roll small pieces of marzipan into sausages roughly the length of the centre of each date and fill the dates with these. Press the toasted almonds into the surface of the marzipan to decorate. Store in an airtight container or tin in a cool place for up to a week.

Makes
45

CHESTNUT BRANDY BALLS

Chestnuts are commonly made into confections in southern Europe and make a strongly aromatic and tender filling for these winter truffles.

Time: I hour plus 4 hours
  freezing and resting time

250g cooked chestnuts
75g icing sugar
I tbsp brandy
seeds from I vanilla pod
300g best-quality dark
  chocolate, chopped into
  small pieces

You'll also need
Vinyl gloves
Chocolate dipping fork or
  other small fork with fine
  tines

Place the chestnuts in the bowl of a food processor and purée until very smooth. Tip the purée into a large bowl and knead in the icing sugar, brandy and vanilla seeds. Allow the mixture to set for an hour, then shape the mixture into small balls. Freeze for a couple of hours to harden completely.

When the chestnut balls are completely frozen, melt 50g of the chocolate in a small heatproof bowl in a microwave. Have ready a sheet of non-stick baking paper on a clean tray.

Remove the chestnut balls from the freezer, don your vinyl gloves and coat each with a fine layer of the chocolate by placing some chocolate on the palm of one hand, and rolling the balls in it using the other. Place the balls onto the paper-lined tray. Rest the balls at room temperature for I–2 hours to allow any condensation to evaporate.

When you are ready to finish the chocolates, melt the remaining chocolate in a small heatproof bowl in the microwave. If you want a particularly shiny and crisp coating, temper the chocolate according to the instructions on page 150.

Dip the chocolates one at a time into the melted chocolate using a dipping fork, tapping the fork on the edge of the bowl to remove excess chocolate and carefully place upside-down on a tray lined with clean baking paper.

As you work, you will find that the chocolate will cool, so you may need to re-warm it briefly in the microwave to liquefy it. The amount of chocolate you ultimately use will depend on how runny it is.

Note: It is important that the balls come up to room temperature once they have had their first coating of chocolate; if they are still cold, or if you are working in a cold room, the second coating may crack. If this happens, simply re-dip the chocolates in a final layer of chocolate.

Makes
25

HONEY SESAME SQUARES

Heating the honey intensifies the flavour, which is balanced by the nuttiness of the toasted sesame seeds. Be sure to pay attention as the final mixture boils, as it will burn easily.

Time: 40 minutes

250g sesame seeds
310g honey, preferably
  heather honey
2 tsp lemon juice

You'll also need
24 x 18cm baking tray
Temperature probe or
  sugar thermometer

Line the baking tray with non-stick baking paper.

Toast the sesame seeds by placing them in a dry frying pan over a low to medium heat and tossing them until they are lightly browned.

Add the seeds to a medium pan along with the honey and lemon juice. Bring to a simmer over a medium heat, stirring, and then cook until the mixture reaches 138–140°C. Pour the syrup immediately into the prepared tin and shake the tin carefully to encourage the mixture to settle. As it cools, you can press the surface down with a lightly oiled palette knife to consolidate the mixture into an even, flat layer.

When the mixture is cold, cut into 3cm squares using a sharp knife. Store, layered between sheets of non-stick baking paper in an airtight container or tin in a cool place. Eat within a week.

Makes about 800g

PINE NUT SWEETS

Chewy and protein rich, pine nuts make an unusual addition to this cooked confection. The mixture is split into two portions, one of which is flavoured with cocoa – you can then cut each portion into lozenges and pile them attractively together to serve.

Time: 35 minutes

500g granulated sugar
150ml water
¼ tsp cream of tartar
400g pine nuts
½ tbsp plain flour
40g cocoa powder

You'll also need
Large silicone non-stick
  baking mat
Temperature probe or
  sugar thermometer

Before you cook the sweets, put the silicone mat onto a large tray and place it near the cooker.

Place the sugar, water and cream of tartar in a medium pan set on a low heat. Cook, stirring to dissolve the sugar, then raise the heat to medium-high and stop stirring. Use a pastry brush dipped in hot water to wash down the insides of the pan to prevent any crystals forming. Boil until the temperature reaches 116°C, then remove the pan from the heat and stand it on a heatproof surface. Add the pine nuts and the flour. Mix well, then pour half the mixture on to one side of the silicone mat. Add the cocoa powder to the other half of the mix and stir to combine. Pour the cocoa mixture on to the other half of the mat, not touching the other mixture. Use an oiled palette knife to flatten each portion of the mixture into an even rectangle about 1cm deep.

When the mixture is cold, cut it into small diamonds and store in an airtight container or tin in between sheets of non-stick baking paper.

Makes about 500g

CHOCOLATE BRAZILS

You can use your favourite chocolate for coating these waxy nuts; just remember that you will only achieve a fine result if you use couverture (see page 16).

Time: 35 minutes

200g best-quality milk chocolate, chopped into small pieces
300g finest quality brazil nuts (shelled weight)

You'll also need
Chocolate dipping fork or small fork with fine tines

Melt the chocolate by placing the chocolate in a heatproof bowl in a microwave. Pulse for 15-second blasts, stirring in between until the chocolate is fully melted and runny. If you want to temper the chocolate to make it particularly shiny and hard, follow the instructions on page 150.

Have ready a tray lined with non-stick baking paper. Drop the nuts two or three at a time into the chocolate and use a dipping fork to enrobe the nuts before lifting them out, tapping gently on the side of the bowl and placing carefully on the paper-lined tray.

As you work, you will find that the chocolate will cool, so you may need to re-warm it briefly in the microwave to liquefy it. The amount of chocolate you ultimately use will depend on how runny it is.

When the nuts are all coated, leave them to cool until set at room temperature, then store in a cool place in an airtight container or tin.

Makes
50

ALMOND, CHOCOLATE HONEY HEARTS

These little biscuits are a perfect accompaniment to an after-dinner coffee – crisp and scented with orange flower water and honey. Why not try making a batch for a Valentine's treat?

Time: 1½ hours

225g flaked almonds
25g plain flour
Pinch sea salt flakes
  (preferably Maldon)
150g granulated sugar
50g demerara sugar
45g honey
50ml double cream
110g unsalted butter
1 tbsp orange flower water
150g dark chocolate,
  chopped into small pieces
Sunflower or almond oil,
  for greasing

You'll also need
2 silicone moulds with
  50 small heart-shaped
  holes in total

Preheat the oven to 175°C/325°F/Gas mark 3. Grease the silicone moulds carefully with a little oil, brushing or wiping it into the corners very carefully. Place each of the moulds on a baking tray.

Put three quarters of the flaked almonds into the bowl of a food processor, add the flour and pulse the mixture until the almonds are reduced but not to a powder – just enough to break most of the pieces up. Tip them into a bowl and mix with the remaining almonds and the salt, stirring to mix.

Place the sugars, honey, cream and butter in a medium pan over a low heat, stirring to dissolve the sugars. Raise the heat to medium-high and cook until the syrup reaches 114°C. Remove from the heat and stir in the nuts and orange flower water.

Place a cherry-sized ball of the mixture into each heart-shaped hole and bake for 10–15 minutes until the mixture is an even mid-brown all over. Continue to cook the hearts in batches until you have used up all the mixture, cooling the finished hearts on a wire rack.

Melt the chocolate in a heatproof bowl in a microwave, and spread the chocolate on the smooth underside of each heart using a small palette knife. Cool, chocolate side up, on a wire rack until the chocolate is set, and store in an airtight container or tin.

Makes
40–50

HAZELNUT PRALINES

Toasted hazelnuts are ground into a fine powder before being added to a classic ganache, which is then dipped in fine dark chocolate in a recipe that derives from Belgium.

Time: 1½ hours plus a little
  cooling time

100g peeled hazelnuts (see
  page 124)
375ml double cream
375g best-quality dark
  chocolate, chopped into
  small pieces
1 tbsp brandy
1 tbsp honey
200–300g best-quality milk
  chocolate, chopped into
  small pieces
2 tbsp cocoa powder

You'll also need
Melon baller, for shaping the
  centres
Dipping fork or other small
  fork with fine tines

Preheat the oven to 140°C/275°F/Gas mark 1.

Place the hazelnuts on a baking tray and roast for 25–30 minutes, or until the nuts are mid-brown throughout – break a nut in half to check that they are cooked through, otherwise they won't develop their full flavour. Check the nuts from time to time and carefully remove any that are colouring quickly.

When the nuts are cooked, cool them on a clean tray then grind them to a fine powder in a pestle and mortar or food processor.

Heat the cream in a small pan over a medium heat. When it begins to simmer, remove it from the heat and add the chocolate, brandy and honey. Leave for 1 minute, then stir the mixture until it is even and smooth. Add the nut powder and stir to combine. Set the mixture in a small plastic container to cool at room temperature. When the mixture is firm, use a melon baller dipped in boiling water to make even spheres, placing them on a clean tray. Leave to dry, uncovered, for an hour or so.

When the balls are nicely dry, melt the chocolate by placing it in a heatproof bowl in a microwave. Pulse for 15-second blasts, stirring in between until the chocolate is fully melted and runny. If you want to temper the chocolate to make it shiny and hard, follow the instructions on page 150.

Have ready a tray lined with non-stick baking paper. Dip the balls one at a time into the melted chocolate so that they are completely coated, tapping the fork on the side of the bowl to remove excess chocolate, then deposit the balls upside-down on the prepared tray. When the chocolate is still soft, dust the chocolates with cocoa powder and roll them in it to coat entirely.

As you work, you will find that the chocolate will cool, so you may need to re-warm it briefly in the microwave to liquefy it again. The amount of chocolate you ultimately use will depend on how runny it is.

Store in an airtight container or tin in a cool place, and eat within a week.

Makes
36–42

ALMOND, CITRUS AND CHOCOLATE LAYERS

Take your time to prepare this complex layered sweet – the final result will be well worth the effort.

Time: 2 hours plus overnight
setting time

—

150g ground almonds
150g icing sugar
1 egg yolk
1 tbsp brandy
75g candied orange or
grapefruit peel (see recipe
on page 113 or buy the
best you can find)
100g double cream
375g dark chocolate (at least
60% cocoa solids), chopped
into small pieces

You'll also need
Chocolate dipping fork or
small fork with fine tines

Make the marzipan by mixing the almonds and icing sugar in a large bowl, then mixing in the egg yolk and just enough brandy to form a firm dough. Knead lightly, and then transfer to a sheet of non-stick baking paper laid on a work surface. Place another sheet of baking paper on top. Roll the marzipan out to a neat rectangle approximately 5mm thick, using your fingers to help shape neat corners.

Remove the top layer of baking paper, chop the candied peel into short, thin strips and lay these evenly over the surface of the marzipan, pressing them in lightly.

To make the ganache layer, heat the cream in a small pan until it is just steaming. Remove it from the heat and tip in 125g of the chocolate. Leave for 1 minute and then stir to combine. Cool for 5 minutes and then spread evenly over the peel layer with a palette knife.

Allow the layers to set for 1 hour in a cool room. When firm and dry to the touch, cut into even 2.5cm squares. Use a palette knife to transfer the squares to a clean piece of non-stick baking paper set on a tray. Allow the squares to set for an hour or overnight at room temperature, lightly covered with a piece of baking paper. Do not refrigerate or the sweets will go sticky.

When the squares are firm, melt the remaining 250g chocolate by placing it in a heatproof bowl in a microwave. Pulse for 15-second blasts, stirring in between until the chocolate is fully melted and runny. If you want to temper the chocolate to make it particularly shiny and hard, follow the instructions on page 150.

Before dipping the chocolates, have ready a clean tray lined with baking paper.

Use a small fine fork or chocolate dipping fork to dip each square in the melted chocolate. Scrape the underside briefly on the edge of the chocolate bowl and transfer to the clean tray. As you work, you will find that the chocolate will cool, so you may need to re-warm the chocolate to liquefy it. The amount of chocolate you ultimately use will depend on how runny it is.

Leave to set before eating, and then store in an airtight container or tin in a cool place, but not the fridge. These will keep for a week.

Makes
300g

SUGARED ALMONDS

Sugared or crystallised nuts and seeds were popular in the Tudor court, and would traditionally have been made in a shallow copper dish set over a flame. The nuts are cooked in a hot sugar syrup that is stirred to cause crystals to form and this sticks to the hot nuts. The resulting sugar-encrusted nuts are delicious.

Time: 1 hour

300g granulated sugar
75ml water
300g whole unblanched
  almonds

Line a large baking tray with non-stick baking paper.

Place the sugar and water in a heavy frying pan set on a medium heat. Heat, stirring until the mixture boils. Use a pastry brush dipped in hot water to wash down the insides of the pan to prevent crystallisation.

Continue to cook the syrup until it reaches 113°C, then remove it from the heat. Add the almonds and stir the mixture until the syrup begins to cloud and crystallise – this will take several minutes. When the sugar appears dry, tip the mixture into a large colander set over a tray to collect the loose sugar. Return the sugar to the pan and allow it to melt to form a light caramel. Tip in the almonds and remove from the heat. Stir the almonds until the sugar crystallises once again. Repeat this complete procedure again to coat the almonds with as much sugar as possible, then finally tip the nuts onto the prepared tray and allow them to cool fully before storing in an airtight container or tin for up to a week.

Makes
40–50

TURRÓN

I like to use lime honey in this traditional hard form of nougat – it lends the confection a delicious aromatic flavour from the heart of the Mediterranean. The deep flavour of toasted hazelnuts only makes this even more delicious.

Time: 1 hour

100g hazelnuts
Two 20 x 30cm sheets
  edible wafer or rice paper
600g granulated sugar
60g lime honey
25g liquid glucose
100ml water
3 egg whites – 90g
Sunflower or almond oil,
  for greasing

You'll also need
2 icing rulers or pieces of
  wood about 30cm long
  and 1cm square
Temperature probe or
  sugar thermometer

Preheat the oven to 150°C/300°F/Gas mark 2.

Place the hazelnuts on a baking sheet and bake in the oven for 25–30 minutes until golden throughout – break a nut in half to check that they are cooked through, otherwise they won't develop their full flavour. Set aside and allow them to cool, then remove the skins by rubbing the nuts in a clean tea towel, shaking the cleaned nuts into a small bowl.

While the nuts are in the oven, place one sheet of wafer paper on a clean, odour-free chopping board and line up the icing rulers or pieces of wood alongside. Lightly grease these (but not the paper) with sunflower or almond oil.

Place the sugar, honey, liquid glucose and water in a medium pan and place on a low to medium heat until the mixture simmers and the sugar is all dissolved. Let the mixture simmer gently, brushing down the insides of the pan with the pastry brush dipped in hot water to prevent any crystals forming.

Once the syrup reaches 132°C, remove it from the heat and turn your mixer to high to start beating the egg whites. As soon as they reach soft peaks, pour the honey syrup down the side of the bowl and beat the mixture until it is fully incorporated, then turn your mixer to low and continue to beat the mixture until it is thick and glossy. Check the temperature from time to time – and when it cools to 80°C, turn off the mixer and scrape the mixture from the whisk.

Working quickly now, add the nuts and mix, then pile the nougat onto the wafer paper you prepared earlier. Place the second sheet of wafer paper on top and press or roll the nougat into a rough rectangle using the rulers or pieces of wood as a thickness guide. Take care as the nougat will be very hot.

Allow the mixture to cool for 2–3 hours before cutting it into lengths about 4cm wide. Wrap these in cling film and cut the nougat with a lightly oiled knife into small pieces only when ready to serve.

Store in an airtight container or tin in a cool place for up to a week.

Makes
40–50

ORANGINES

The combination of orange and almonds in these little biscuits is wonderful and they are particularly delicious served with a cup of Earl Grey tea.

Time: 1 hour

55g flaked almonds
55g candied orange peel
  (see page 113) or buy the
  best you can find
Finely grated zest of 1
  medium orange, plus a
  little juice
40g plain flour
55g unsalted butter, softened
55g caster sugar
1 tbsp milk
55g icing sugar

You'll also need
Piping bag fitted with a
  small plain nozzle

Place the almonds, candied peel, zest and flour into the bowl of a food processor and pulse the mixture until the almonds are reduced to small pieces, but are not reduced to a powder.

Tip the mixture into a bowl and add the butter, caster sugar and milk. Knead the mixture to form a smooth dough. Place the mixture onto a sheet of cling film and roll this into a long sausage 2–3cm in diameter. Chill the log in the fridge for an hour until it is firm.

To cook, preheat the oven to 170°C/325°F/Gas mark 3. Line several baking trays with non-stick baking paper, slice the log very thinly and place slices spaced well apart on the trays. Bake in the oven for 10–15 minutes until evenly golden brown. If you notice that the edges are beginning to brown quickly, reduce the heat slightly so that the orangines colour evenly. Cool on a wire rack and continue to bake the mixture until you have used it all up.

Make a thick icing using the icing sugar and a very little orange juice. Place in a piping bag and decorate the smooth undersides of the orangines with a swirl of icing. Alternatively, use a small knife to spread a little icing onto them.

Store between layers of non-stick baking paper in an airtight tin in a cool place for up to a week.

Makes
300g

ALMOND OR MACADAMIA NUT BRITTLE

Fresh almonds would have been a seasonal treat for Isabella, appearing on her table strewn over fresh raisins as part of a dessert. This simple confection uses her caramel recipe, adding in nuts to give a pleasing combination.

Time: 45 minutes

60g blanched almonds or
  macadamia nuts (see
  page 124)
250g granulated sugar
70ml water
Pinch cream of tartar
Sunflower or almond oil,
  for greasing

You'll also need
Large silicone non-stick
  baking mat (optional)
Temperature probe or sugar
  thermometer

Preheat the oven to 150°C/300°F/Gas mark 2. Set the silicone mat on a large baking tray or lightly grease a large baking tray with oil. Half fill your sink with cold water as you will need to cool the base of the pan.

Place the almonds on a baking sheet and bake in the oven for 20 minutes until golden.

Place the sugar, water and cream of tartar in a medium pan and allow the sugar to start dissolving into the water for 5 minutes. Transfer the pan to a low heat and stir until the sugar is dissolved. Raise the heat and bring the mixture to the boil. Stop stirring at this stage. Use a pastry brush dipped in hot water to wash down the sides of the pan to remove any crystals of sugar, which would otherwise ruin your recipe.

Cook the mixture until the syrup reaches 165–170°C, then dip the base of the pan in the water-filled sink for a couple of seconds to arrest the cooking process. Transfer to a heatproof surface and add the almonds, stir to combine and then pour the mixture out onto the non-stick baking sheet so that it forms a thin layer. You can, should you like, pop another non-stick baking sheet on top and press it down to make an even layer. Cool until the mixture is set and crisp, then break into rough pieces. Store in an airtight container or tin, where it will keep for up to 1 month in a cool, dark place.

CHOCOLATE

Chocolate is not only delicious as a treat in its own right; it's also incredibly useful to the confectioner as a coating, lining or when combined with cream to create a luxurious filling for truffles.

It is perfectly possible to make your own chocolates at home with no special equipment at all, but if you want to invest a little time and money, you can make very professional-looking filled chocolates that will impress your friends and family.

The perfectly smooth and delicate chocolate that we can buy today for our own sweets is a relatively recent invention. For most of the past 500 years, chocolate was more often used as a drink than as a confection because, to make truly excellent chocolate, a certain amount of technology is required.

During the early part of the 19th century, advances in chocolate manufacture meant that blocks of chocolate, or bars, could be produced. In Britain, Fry and Cadbury – names we are familiar with today – were early pioneers of chocolate eating bars.

At the time Isabella was writing her book, chocolate bars were still a rare and expensive treat. She mentions in the *Book of Household Management* that chocolate should play a part in the dessert course, presented in a fine ornamental box.

It was the Swiss, however, who began to perfect the art of making fine chocolate using machinery that ground the cocoa beans to an incredibly fine paste. They are also accredited with developing the first milk chocolate in the late 1870s.

You can readily buy good chocolate today: dark, milk and white chocolate can all be used to make truffles, and to some extent they are interchangeable, especially so when used as a coating Each type has its own characteristics however and if you want to make good chocolates, it is well worth taking a little time to understand what these are (see page 16). If you want to make fine chocolates, a high-quality cook's chocolate is best (see page 17).

TIPS AND TECHNIQUES

Virtually all the recipes in this chapter involve melting chocolate for enrobing flavoured centres, or for filling moulds, and so it is useful to understand a little about how chocolate behaves when heated and the most foolproof ways of doing so. If you wish to take your chocolate making to the next level, you can learn to temper the chocolate to give a really professional finish. All the techniques you require are detailed below.

MELTING CHOCOLATE

Chocolate will melt at a relatively low temperature – around 25–30°C, depending on the type of chocolate. Milk and white chocolate melt at a lower temperature than dark, so pay particular attention as you heat these because once they are overheated, and burnt, there is nothing you can do to recover the situation.

Chocolate needs to be heated with care. Any humidity caused, for example by melting it in a bowl over a pan of hot water, can cause the chocolate to 'seize', meaning that it will solidify while still hot. This can happen alarmingly quickly, and the chocolate can only then be salvaged if the recipe involves melting the chocolate with butter, as in the case of a chocolate brownie.

A safer, less conventional way to melt chocolate slowly – and my preferred way – is to heat it in the microwave.

Microwave method

Before you heat the chocolate, make sure that the microwave is free from moisture by turning the microwave on empty for 30 seconds, then dry the surfaces with a clean tea towel to remove any condensation. Place the chopped chocolate in a heatproof container and pulse for 15-second bursts on a medium setting. Between each pulse, simply stir the chocolate to ensure that it heats, and melts, evenly. Once melted, the chocolate can simply be pulsed for a few seconds at a time if you require it to remain melted for any period.

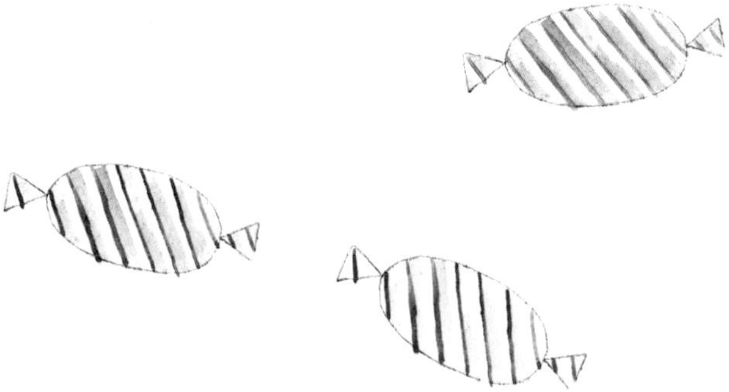

Bain-marie method

If you do not have a microwave, you can melt the chopped chocolate in a bowl set over a pan of hot – not simmering – water, but you must take great care that no water, or steam, comes into contact with the chocolate. This will ruin your recipe, because seized chocolate can never be re-melted on its own.

DIFFERENT TYPES OF FINE CHOCOLATES

Truffles

These are the simplest type of chocolate you can make at home, involving a flavoured cream and chocolate mixture known as ganache. In order to create a deliciously soft filling, the ganache can be frozen in balls, which are then dipped or rolled in melted or tempered chocolate of the same, or contrasting, colour. Occasionally, a recipe will advise you to double-dip the chocolates. This is because occasionally tempered chocolate contracts so much when it cools that it will squeeze some of the filling out of the thin shell. A second dip will cover up any irregularities.

Moulded chocolates

A large variety of moulds are available, from simple silicone ones through to polycarbonate and magnetic moulds for use with transfer sheets that allow you to print designs onto the surface of your chocolates. Moulds such as these are great fun to experiment with. Suppliers are listed at the back of the book.

TEMPERING CHOCOLATE

You'll need
At least 500g best-quality
 or couverture chocolate,
 chopped into small pieces
Spatula temperature probe
 or digital probe (see page
 19)
Palette knife or scraper
Large silicone non-stick mat

This technique involves the careful heating and cooling of chocolate to specific temperatures to create beautifully shiny crisp chocolate that is perfect for fine truffles and bars.

When you buy chocolate in the form of a bar, or button, it is said to be 'in temper'. This is a particular state that chocolate achieves when all of the cocoa butter crystals are stable, known as beta form. In this state, the chocolate is brittle, snaps easily and will shine. When we melt chocolate at home, we take it out of temper – i.e. above the temperature where large undesirable crystals form, and so in order to create perfect chocolates at home, we must temper it.

Essentially, the technique involves heating the chocolate to melt it and to completely liquefy the crystals of cocoa butter, then cooling it before reheating slightly to a specific temperature, as outlined below.

You will find it easier to work with a large quantity of chocolate as it will hold its temperature for longer (1–2kg is easier to handle than a small amount). You may have chocolate left over – that is fine as you can keep any remaining chocolate for a later recipe.

There is no mystery to it, just the need to keep a careful eye on the temperature. The technique is described below and is the same for each type of chocolate other than there are slight variations in temperature for milk and white chocolates, which must be adhered to.

At all times ensure that your surfaces and tools are perfectly clean and dry.

Step 1

Melt the chocolate in a clean, dry microwave using short blasts as described on page 148, and once the chocolate is beginning to liquefy, measure the temperature using a probe and continue to slowly increase the temperature until you reach 45°C for dark and 40°C for milk and white chocolate.

Step 2

Cool the chocolate to 28°C for dark and milk chocolate; 25°C for white. To do this quickly, simple pour the chocolate out onto a silicone non-stick mat or scrupulously clean and dry surface, spreading it out with a palette knife or scraper. As you stir the chocolate, keep monitoring its temperature with a probe – it cools quickly, so when it has reached the desired temperature, simply scrape it into a clean pre-warmed bowl and reheat as directed below.

Step 3

Heat the chocolate in 2–3 second blasts in the microwave to its final working temperature:
* Dark – 32°C
* Milk – 30°C
* White – 28°C

Tempered chocolate sets quickly, so ensure that you have everything you need in place to finish your chocolates. If you have chocolate left over, simply spread it out on a sheet of non-stick baking paper to set, then break it into small pieces which will re-melt easily next time. You will need to re-temper the chocolate each time you use it.

Makes
700g

CHOCOLATE HONEYCOMB

I like to use a mild English honey for this recipe, but you can use whichever is your favourite. Remember, though, that when the honey is cooked, the flavour will intensify.

Time: 2 hours including
   1 hour to cool
—
330g granulated sugar
120g liquid glucose
140g lightly flavoured honey
80ml water
40g bicarbonate of soda
200g best-quality dark
   chocolate, chopped into
   small pieces

You'll also need
20 x 30cm baking tray
Temperature probe or sugar
   thermometer
Dipping fork, or other small
   fork with fine tines

Line the baking tin with non-stick baking paper.

Place the sugar, liquid glucose, honey and water in a large saucepan (this should have high sides as the mixture will bubble up greatly when the bicarbonate of soda is added) and stir this over a medium heat until the sugar has dissolved. Raise the heat to high and boil the syrup until it reaches 165°C. Use a pastry brush dipped in hot water to wash down the insides of the pan to dissolve any crystals that might form. Immediately remove the pan from the heat and whisk in the bicarbonate of soda. The mixture will bubble up and expand quickly. Pour it quickly into your prepared tin and allow it to set for an hour or two in a warm dry place until it is firm.

Break the honeycomb into pieces the size of a walnut by tapping it gently with a large spoon or toffee hammer.

Melt the chocolate in a heatproof bowl in a microwave. Be careful not to overheat it (see page 150 for notes on melting and tempering chocolate).

Working quickly, dip the pieces of honeycomb into the melted chocolate using a dipping fork and transfer them to a tray lined with baking paper. As you work you may find the chocolate thickens as it cools, so you may need to re-warm the chocolate by briefly pulsing it in the microwave. The actual amount of chocolate you use depends on how liquid it is when you dip. If you have any leftover, store in an airtight container or tin in a cool place, but not in the fridge.

Makes
40

FRUIT AND
NUT CLUSTERS

You can use a wide selection of fruits and nuts in this recipe, so long as the pieces are cut into similar sizes – just don't increase the total weight or you won't have enough chocolate to stick them together.

Time: I hour plus 2 hours
  cooling

100g blanched almonds
50g peeled hazelnuts
100g raisins or sultanas
50g candied orange or
  grapefruit peel (see page
  113 or buy the best you
  can find), chopped into
  small pieces
350g dark chocolate,
  chopped into small pieces

You'll also need
Chocolate dipping fork,
  or other small fork with
  fine tines

Preheat the oven to 140°C/275°F/Gas mark 1.

Place the almonds and hazelnuts on separate trays and toast in the oven for 25–30 minutes. Check the nuts from time to time and remove any that appear to be colouring too quickly. They should be a rich golden to mid-brown colour throughout – break a nut in half to check that they are cooked to the centre. Allow the nuts to cool while you prepare the other ingredients.

Place the raisins and candied peel in a large bowl. Melt 150g of the dark chocolate in a small heatproof bowl in a microwave, pulsing it in 15-second blasts, stirring in between each pulse. Add the cooled nuts to the raisins and thoroughly mix in the melted chocolate.

Place a sheet of non-stick baking paper on a tray. Using a teaspoon, deposit chunks of the chocolate nut mixture on the tray. Allow these to cool fully for an hour or so until they are firm.

Line a second tray with baking paper, and melt the remaining 200g chocolate in a small bowl in a small heatproof bowl in a microwave, pulsing it in 15-second blasts, stirring in between each pulse. If you want a particularly shiny and hard finish, follow the instructions on page 150 for tempering chocolate.

Using a dipping fork, dip the firm chocolate chunks into the melted chocolate, tap to remove excess chocolate, then deposit the finished chocolates onto a clean tray lined with baking paper to set. Store in an airtight container or tin.

Makes
30

CHOCOLATE GINGERS

Isabella mentions in her Book of Household Management *that ginger is frequently handed round after ices, to prepare the palette for dessert wine. Crystallised ginger is easy to make and even better when dipped in dark chocolate as in the recipe here. Alternatively, you can buy 200g good-quality crystallised ginger and skip to the dipping part of the recipe.*

Time: 1½ hour

1kg plump fresh ginger root
800g–1kg granulated sugar
200ml water
200g best-quality dark
  chocolate, chopped into
  small pieces

You'll also need
Chocolate dipping fork or
  small fork with fine tines

Peel the ginger carefully with the tip of a teaspoon or a very sharp knife. Rinse the ginger, and cut it into 5–10mm slices.

Put the ginger slices into a large pan and add enough boiling water to cover it by 1cm. Bring to a gentle simmer and allow the ginger to cook until it is tender: depending on the freshness of the ginger, this will take 20–40 minutes. Drain off the water and leave the ginger to drain fully in a colander suspended over a large bowl to catch any drips.

Weigh out the ginger and an equal amount of sugar. Place the sugar in a large wide-bottomed pan with 200ml water and leave for a few minutes to allow the dissolving process to start gently. Add the ginger and stir the mixture over a low heat with a clean wooden spoon. As the mixture begins to cook, and the sugar dissolves, stir it constantly and when the sugar has dissolved, increase the heat so that the mixture begins to simmer and boil. Reduce the heat to low and simmer, stirring for around 30 minutes until all the syrup has reduced to a bare minimum. As the ginger cools it will begin to crystallise and dry. Lift out the ginger and spread it on a clean cooling rack or a sheet of non-stick baking paper to dry, turning occasionally. Store in an airtight tin when completely cooled.

Weigh out 200g of the candied ginger ready for dipping. Use a pastry brush to remove any excess sugar from the pieces of ginger.

Melt the chocolate in a heatproof bowl in a microwave. Be careful not to overheat it (see page 150 for notes on melting and tempering chocolate).

Working quickly, dip each of the pieces of ginger in the melted chocolate using a dipping fork and transfer them to a tray lined with non-stick baking paper. As you work you may find the chocolate thickens as it cools, so you may need to re-warm the chocolate by briefly pulsing it in the microwave. The actual amount of chocolate you use depends on how liquid it is when you dip. If you have any leftover, store it in a cool place (not the fridge) until you need it.

Makes
300g

CHOCOLATE MINT CRISPS

Little mint chocolate bars with crispy mint crystals are lovely as an after-dinner treat with coffee.

Time: 10 minutes plus 1
  hour to cool

100g demerara sugar
½ tsp peppermint extract
200g best-quality dark
  chocolate, chopped into
  small pieces

You'll also need
18 x 24cm baking tray

Line the baking tray with non-stick baking paper.

Mix the demerara sugar and peppermint extract together in a small bowl.

Melt the chocolate in a heatproof bowl in a microwave. Be careful not to overheat it (see page 150 for notes on melting and tempering chocolate).

Mix the mint sugar into the chocolate, and pour this into the prepared tray. Tilt the tray to encourage the chocolate to spread out, and tap it gently to settle it. Allow the chocolate to cool at room temperature.

When the chocolate is completely set, lift it onto a clean cutting board and score it into even pieces with a sharp knife. Carefully transfer the pieces into a tin, layered between pieces of non-stick baking paper.

SILVERED ORANGE SLICES

Edible silver leaf can be used to make a really special gift of crystallised orange slices. If you are a fan of chocolate-orange flavours then you could also try dipping candied peel (see page 113) in melted dark chocolate.

Time: 30 minutes

200g candied orange slices
  (see recipe on page 114)
150g best-quality dark
  chocolate, chopped into
  small pieces
4–5 pages silver leaf

You'll also need
Small fine paintbrush

Scrape any excess sugar crystals from the orange slices and cut them in half.

Have ready a large tray lined with non-stick baking paper.

Melt the chocolate in a small heatproof bowl in a microwave, pulsing for 15-second blasts and stirring in between each pulse.

If you want a particularly shiny and hard finish, follow the instructions for tempering chocolate on page 150.

Dip one half of each slice of orange in the chocolate, shake to remove any excess chocolate and place on the paper-lined tray.

While the chocolate is still tacky, use a small fine brush to deposit small pieces of the silver leaf onto each piece.

Store the slices in between layers of non-stick baking paper in an airtight tin.

Makes
25

SIMPLE CHOCOLATE TRUFFLES

This is one of the easiest chocolate recipes that absolutely relies on the best-quality chocolate, as its flavour will really shine through.

Time: I hour plus 2 hours
 cooling

125g best-quality dark
 chocolate, chopped into
 small pieces
90g unsalted butter
I tbsp water
I tbsp caster sugar
I egg yolk
Cocoa powder, for rolling
 – about 2 tbsp

You'll also need
Melon baller

Melt the chocolate in a small heatproof bowl in a microwave, pulsing it in 15-second blasts, stirring in between each pulse. When it has melted fully, stir in the butter, then add the water, caster sugar and egg yolk. Stir the mixture to combine, and cool at room temperature until the mixture is firm.

Use a melon baller dipped in hot water to shape even balls of the mixture. Roll the balls in cocoa powder and place on a tray lined with non-stick baking paper. Store in an airtight container or tin in the fridge and eat within a week.

RUM TRUFFLES

If you like a strong rum flavour, use a dark Barbados rum in this recipe, or a lighter Jamaican one for a more subtle flavour.

Time: I hour plus 2 hours
  cooling

125g best-quality chocolate,
  chopped into small pieces
30g butter
I tbsp icing sugar
2 egg yolks
2 tsp rum
Seeds from ½ vanilla pod
Cocoa powder, for rolling
  – about 2 tbsp

You'll also need
Melon baller

Melt the chocolate in a small heatproof bowl in a microwave, pulsing it in 15-second blasts, stirring in between each pulse. When it has melted fully, stir in the butter, then add the rum, icing sugar and egg yolks. Stir the mixture to combine, and cool at room temperature until the mixture is firm.

Use a melon baller dipped in hot water to shape even balls of the mixture. Roll the balls in cocoa powder and place on a tray lined with non-stick baking paper. Store in an airtight container or tin and eat within a week.

Makes
30–35

VANILLA CREAM TRUFFLES

A simple truffle that uses real vanilla pods to enhance the natural flavours of the chocolate in the ganache filling.

Time: 1 hour cooking plus
overnight chilling and
freezing

150ml double cream
Seeds from 2 vanilla pods
150g best-quality dark
chocolate
300g best-quality white
chocolate, chopped into
small pieces

You'll also need
Chocolate dipping fork or
small fork with fine tines
Vinyl gloves

Place the cream in a small saucepan, add the vanilla seeds and bring to a simmer. Remove the pan from the heat and add the chocolate. Leave for 1 minute, then stir to combine. Transfer the mixture to a small container and allow it to chill in the fridge for an hour or two. When the ganache is firm, use a melon baller dipped in hot water to shape even spheres. Place these on a clean tray lined with non-stick baking paper and cover with cling film. Freeze for an hour or overnight.

Bring the ganache balls out of the freezer. Melt 50g white chocolate in a small heatproof bowl and don your vinyl gloves. Have ready a second tray lined with non-stick baking paper. Place a little chocolate in the palm of one hand and roll each ball in the chocolate using your fingers so that each has a fine coating of chocolate. Place these on the tray to set – this will happen very quickly. Set the balls aside at room temperature for 1–2 hours to come up to room temperature.

When you are ready to finish the truffles, melt the remaining white chocolate in a heatproof bowl in a microwave. Be careful not to overheat it (see page 150 for notes on melting and tempering chocolate).

Working quickly, dip each of the ganache balls in the melted chocolate using a dipping fork and transfer them to a tray lined with baking paper. As you work you may find the chocolate thickens as it cools, so you may need to re-warm the chocolate by briefly pulsing it in the microwave. The actual amount of chocolate you use depends on how liquid it is when you dip.

Allow the truffles to come up to room temperature before transferring to an airtight container or tin to store. Eat within a week and store in a cool place, but do not store in the fridge.

Note: It is important that the balls come up to room temperature once they have had their first coating of chocolate; if they are still cold, or if you are working in a cold room, the second coating may crack. If this happens, do not worry; simply re-dip the chocolates in a final layer of chocolate.

PISTACHIO TRUFFLES

The best deep green pistachios come from Sicily and can be bought from specialist grocers or from the suppliers listed on page 202.

Time: 2 hours plus 1–2
hours chilling and freezing

25g Sicilian pistachios
100ml double cream
150g best-quality white
  chocolate, chopped into
  small pieces
200g best-quality dark
  chocolate, chopped into
  small pieces

You'll also need
Melon baller
Chocolate dipping fork
  or other small fork with
  fine tines
Vinyl gloves

Grind the pistachios in a spice grinder or small food processor until the nuts form a slightly oily and very smooth paste.

Heat the cream in a small pan over a medium heat until it just begins to simmer, then remove it from the heat and add the white chocolate. Leave this for 1 minute, then stir until the chocolate is all melted. Add the pistachio paste and then blend with a hand blender for a few seconds to emulsify the mixture. Allow to cool.

To shape the mixture into truffle centres, you can either use a melon baller, in which case you will need to chill the mixture in the fridge until it is firm enough to ball; or you can pipe the mixture into long, 5mm-diameter logs onto a sheet of non-stick baking paper. This can then be frozen until you are ready to cut the logs into short lengths and dip them. Whichever method you chose, you will need to ensure that the mixture is firm enough to dip into melted chocolate without melting.

Bring the centres out of the freezer. Melt 50g dark chocolate in a small heatproof bowl in a microwave and don your vinyl gloves. Have ready a second tray lined with non-stick baking paper. Place a little chocolate in the palm of one hand and roll each centre in the chocolate using your fingers so that each has a fine coating of chocolate. Place these on the tray to set, which will happen very quickly. Set the balls aside in a cool place for an hour or two to come up to room temperature (see Note on page 162).

When you are ready to finish the truffles, melt the remaining chocolate in a heatproof bowl in a microwave. Be careful not to overheat it (see page 150 for notes on melting and tempering chocolate).

Working quickly, dip each of the centres in the melted chocolate using a dipping fork and transfer them to a tray lined with baking paper. As you work you may find the chocolate thickens as it cools, so you may need to re-warm the chocolate by briefly pulsing it in the microwave. The actual amount of chocolate you use depends on how liquid it is when you dip.

Allow the truffles to come up to room temperature before transferring to an airtight container or tin to store. Eat within a week and store in a cool place.

Makes
30–35

CAPPUCCINO TRUFFLES

Ground coffee is used to add powerful flavour to a dark ganache, which is balanced with a coating of sweet, smooth white chocolate.

Time: 1 hour cooking plus
  overnight chilling and
  freezing

150ml double cream
20g finely ground coffee
A little sugar or honey,
  to taste
150g best-quality dark
  chocolate, chopped into
  small pieces
300g best-quality white
  chocolate, chopped into
  small pieces
1 tsp cocoa powder,
  for dusting

You'll also need
Melon baller
Vinyl gloves
Chocolate dipping fork or
  small fork with fine tines
Muslin squares, for straining

Place the cream in a small saucepan and bring to a simmer. Add the coffee and remove from the heat. Steep for 10 minutes, then strain through a muslin-lined sieve into a small pan. Reheat and add a little sugar or honey to taste. When the mixture simmers, remove the pan from the heat and add the chocolate. Leave for 1 minute then stir to combine. Transfer the mixture to a small container and allow it to chill in the fridge for an hour or two. When the ganache is firm, use a melon baller dipped in hot water to shape even spheres. Place these on a clean tray lined with non-stick baking paper and cover with cling film. Freeze for an hour or overnight.

Bring the ganache balls out of the freezer. Melt 50g white chocolate in a small heatproof bowl and don your vinyl gloves. Have ready a second tray lined with non-stick baking paper. Place a little chocolate in the palm of one hand and roll each ball in the chocolate so that each has a fine coating of chocolate. Place these on the tray to set – this will happen very quickly. Set the balls aside at room temperature for an hour or two to come up to room temperature (see Note on page 162).

When you are ready to finish the truffles, melt the remaining white chocolate in a heatproof bowl in a microwave. Be careful not to overheat it (see page 150 for notes on melting and tempering chocolate).

Working quickly, dip each of the ganache balls in the melted chocolate using a dipping fork and transfer them to a tray lined with baking paper. As you work you may find the chocolate thickens as it cools, so you may need to re-warm the chocolate by briefly pulsing it in the microwave.

When the chocolates have all been dipped and have set completely, sprinkle a very small amount of cocoa powder on top of each.

The actual amount of chocolate you use depends on how liquid it is when you dip. If you have any leftover, store it in a cool place until you need it.

Allow the truffles to come up to room temperature before transferring to an airtight container or tin. Eat within a week and store in a cool place, but do not refrigerate.

Makes
25–35

CHAMPAGNE TRUFFLES

Marc de Champagne is a spirit derived from Champagne and is subtle – hence this recipe uses delicately flavoured white chocolate to coat the ganache so that the flavour of the filling comes through.

Time: I hour cooking plus
  overnight chilling and
  freezing
──
130ml double cream
150g best-quality dark
  chocolate, chopped into
  small pieces
20ml Marc de Champagne
I tbsp honey
300g best-quality white
  chocolate, broken into
  pieces

You'll also need
Melon baller
Vinyl gloves
Chocolate dipping fork or
  small fork with fine tines

Heat the cream in a small saucepan over a medium heat. When it begins to simmer, remove from the heat and add the dark chocolate, Marc de Champagne and honey. Leave for I minute, then stir to combine. Transfer the mixture to a small container and allow it to chill in the fridge for an hour or two. When the ganache is firm, use a melon baller dipped in hot water to shape even spheres. Place these on a clean tray lined with non-stick baking paper and cover with cling film. Freeze for an hour or overnight.

Bring the ganache balls out of the freezer. Melt 50g of the white chocolate in a small heatproof bowl and don your vinyl gloves. Have ready a second tray lined with non-stick baking paper. Place a little melted chocolate in the palm of one hand and roll each ball in the chocolate using your fingers so that each has a fine coating of chocolate. Place on the tray to set – this will happen very quickly.

Set the balls aside at room temperature for an hour or two to come up to room temperature (see Note on page 162).

When you are ready to finish the truffles, melt the remaining white chocolate in a heatproof bowl in a microwave. Be careful not to overheat it (see page 150 for notes on melting and tempering white chocolate).

Working quickly, dip each of the ganache balls in the melted chocolate using a dipping fork and transfer them to a tray lined with baking paper. As you work you may find the chocolate thickens as it cools, so you may need to re-warm the chocolate by briefly pulsing it in the microwave.

The actual amount of chocolate you use depends on how liquid it is when you dip. If you have any leftover, store it in a cool place until you need it.

Allow the truffles to come up to room temperature before transferring to an airtight container or tin to store in a cool place. Eat within a week.

Makes
30–35

CRÈME DE VIOLETTE TRUFFLES

Crème de violette is a liqueur produced from the roots of the Parma violet which grows in southern Europe. It is available from online suppliers – see the section at the back of the book.

Time: 1 hour cooking plus overnight chilling and freezing

120ml double cream
30ml crème de violette
450g best-quality dark chocolate, chopped into small pieces

You'll also need
Melon baller
Vinyl gloves
Chocolate dipping fork or small fork with fine tines

Place the cream and crème de violette in a small saucepan and bring to a simmer. Remove the pan from the heat and add 150g of the chocolate. Leave for 1 minute, then stir to combine. Transfer the mixture to a small container and allow it to chill in the fridge for an hour or two. When the ganache is firm, use a melon baller dipped in hot water to shape even spheres. Place these on a clean tray lined with non-stick baking paper and cover with cling film. Freeze for an hour or overnight.

Bring the ganache balls out of the freezer. Melt 50g of the chocolate in a small heatproof bowl and don your vinyl gloves. Have ready a second tray lined with non-stick baking paper. Place a little chocolate in the palm of one hand and roll each ball in the chocolate using your fingers so that each has a fine coating of chocolate. Place these to set on the tray, which will happen very quickly.

Set the balls aside at room temperature for an hour or two to come up to room temperature (see Note on page 162).

When you are ready to finish the truffles, melt the remaining chocolate in a heatproof bowl in a microwave. Be careful not to overheat it (see page 150 for notes on melting and tempering chocolate).

Working quickly, dip each of the ganache balls in the melted chocolate using a dipping fork and transfer them to a tray lined with baking paper. As you work you may find the chocolate thickens as it cools, so you may need to re-warm the chocolate by briefly pulsing it in the microwave. The actual amount of chocolate you use depends on how liquid it is when you dip. If you have any leftover, store it in a cool place until you need it.

Allow the truffles to come up to room temperature before transferring to an airtight container or tin. Eat within a week and store in a cool place, but do not refrigerate.

CHOCOLATE HAZELNUT SALTED CARAMELS

This recipe uses the soft salted caramel filling on page 62 to fill demi-sphere shells of bitter dark chocolate. Only a small amount of the soft caramel is used for the filling, so you could use the remainder for filling a cake, or keep it in the fridge for serving over ice cream.

Time: 2 hours

220g best-quality dark
   chocolate, chopped into
   small pieces
75g Soft Salted Caramel
   (see page 62)
24 hazelnuts, peeled and
   toasted (see page 125)

You'll also need
24-hole polycarbonate
   demi-sphere mould
Temperature probe,
   preferably fast reacting
Disposable piping bag

Set the silicone mat set in a large baking tray.

Temper the chocolate according to the method on page 150.

Fill a large roasting tin with water heated to 32°C and sit a clean bowl in the tin.

First make the chocolate demi-sphere shells: pour the tempered chocolate over the mould, allowing each hole to be completely filled. Tap the mould on your worktop to remove any air bubbles, then invert the mould over your non-stick mat. Shake out the bulk of the melted chocolate, tapping the mould to encourage it to drop out. Return the mould to the right way up and use a metal scraper or palette knife to scrape the surface of the mould completely clean of chocolate.

Put the mould into the fridge for 10 minutes to chill it, but no longer as otherwise you will develop condensation.

Meanwhile, scrape the excess chocolate into a clean bowl set in your water-filled tin.

Maintain the water at as close to 31–32°C as possible until the chocolate sets if you want to keep it in temper, pulsing it in the microwave if necessary for a few seconds.

Pipe a little caramel into each mould, then add a hazelnut to each. Pipe in additional caramel around the nut to come within 2mm or so of the top edge.

Stir the remaining chocolate in its bowl to keep it liquid, then lift the bowl out of the warm water, dry the base of the bowl, and pour the remaining chocolate over the moulds. Holding a metal scraper or palette knife at an angle of 30 degrees or so, scrape quickly over the surface of the mould, pressing firmly against the surface of the mould. Chill the finished chocolates for 10 minutes in the fridge, then remove and allow them to cool fully at room temperature until the chocolate is completely set and hard.

Any chocolate you have leftover can be kept for another recipe.

To extract the chocolates simply tap the mould upside down on a clean tray and the chocolates should pop out. Store in an airtight tin in a cool place, but not the fridge.

Makes
30–35

WHITE CHOCOLATE
& KAHLÚA TRUFFLES

If you love white chocolate, then these are the truffles for you – they are rather like eating a solid white chocolate latte. They complement a cup of after-dinner espresso excellently.

Time: 1 hour cooking plus
   overnight chilling and
   freezing

70ml double cream
Seeds from 1 vanilla pod
450g best-quality white
   chocolate, chopped into
   small pieces
30ml Kahlúa liqueur

You'll also need
Melon baller
Chocolate dipping fork or
   small fork with fine tines

Place the cream in a small saucepan, add the vanilla seeds and bring to a simmer. Remove the pan from the heat and add 150g of the white chocolate along with the Kahlúa. Leave for 1 minute, then stir to combine. Transfer the mixture to a small container and allow it to chill in the fridge for an hour or two. When the ganache is firm, use a melon baller dipped in hot water to shape even spheres. Place these on a clean tray lined with non-stick baking paper and cover with cling film. Freeze for an hour or overnight.

Bring the ganache balls out of the freezer. Melt 50g of the white chocolate in a small heatproof bowl in the microwave and don your vinyl gloves. Have ready a second tray lined with non-stick baking paper. Place a little chocolate in the palm of one hand and roll each ball in the chocolate using your fingers so that each has a fine coating of chocolate. Place these on the tray to set – this will happen very quickly. Set the balls aside for an hour or two to come up to room temperature (see Note on page 162).

When you are ready to finish the truffles, melt the remaining white chocolate in a heatproof bowl in a microwave. Be careful not to overheat it (see page 150 for notes on melting and tempering chocolate).

Working quickly, dip each of the ganache balls in the melted chocolate using a dipping fork and transfer them to a tray lined with baking paper. As you work you may find the chocolate thickens as it cools, so you may need to re-warm the chocolate by briefly pulsing it in the microwave.

The actual amount of chocolate you use depends on how liquid it is when you dip. If you have any leftover, store it in a cool place until you need it.

Allow the truffles to come up to room temperature before transferring them to an airtight container to store in a cool place (do not refrigerate). Eat within a week.

Makes
15

WHITE CHOCOLATE LEMON TRUFFLES

Fresh lemon and orange juice and zest is used in this recipe to lighten the sweet richness of white chocolate.

Time: 2 hours plus 1–2 hours chilling and freezing

Finely grated zest and juice of 1 lemon
Finely grated zest and juice of 1 orange
25g granulated sugar
100ml double cream
225g best-quality white chocolate, chopped into small pieces
25g unsalted butter
200g best-quality dark chocolate, chopped into small pieces

You'll also need
Melon baller
Chocolate dipping fork or small fork with fine tines
Vinyl gloves

Place the fruit juices and sugar into a small pan over a medium heat. Stir to dissolve the sugar and allow the mixture to simmer, then reduce the heat to low and allow the mixture to cook for 5 minutes until it reduces to a thick glossy syrup – you should end up with no more than 50ml.

In a separate pan, warm the cream over a medium heat. Just before it simmers, take the pan off the heat and add the chocolate. Stir until the mixture is smooth. Add the syrup in small quantities, stirring thoroughly, and then beat in the butter. Mix in the citrus zest and use the hand blender to emulsify the mixture. Allow the mixture to cool in a clean bowl at room temperature.

To shape the mixture into truffle centres, you can either use a melon baller, in which case you will need to chill the mixture in the fridge until it is firm enough to ball, or you can pipe the mixture into long, 5mm-diameter logs onto a sheet of non-stick baking paper. If you like, the mixture can be frozen as balls or logs and then you have the option of just dipping a few as and when you need them. Just be sure that the mixture is firm enough to dip into melted chocolate without melting.

Bring the centres out of the freezer. Melt 50g dark chocolate in a small heatproof bowl in a microwave and don your vinyl gloves. Have ready a second tray lined with non-stick baking paper. Place a little chocolate in the palm of one hand and roll each centre in the chocolate using your fingers so that each has a fine coating of chocolate. Place these on the tray to set, which will happen very quickly.

Set the balls aside in a cool place for an hour or two to come up to room temperature (see Note on page 162).

When you are ready to finish the truffles, melt the remaining chocolate in a heatproof bowl in a microwave. Be careful not to overheat it (see page 148).

Working quickly, dip each of the centres in the melted chocolate using a dipping fork and transfer them to a tray lined with baking paper. You may find the chocolate thickens as it cools – just re-warm the chocolate in the microwave. The actual amount of chocolate you use depends on how liquid it is when you dip. If you have any leftover, store it in a cool place until you need it.

Allow the truffles to come up to room temperature before transferring to an airtight container or tin. Eat within a week and store in a cool place but do not refrigerate.

Makes
300g

CHOCOLATE MARSHMALLOW BARS

This easy recipe produces a divine result – a crisp chocolate bar studded with little marshmallow chunks, and a touch of ginger crunch for a treat. You can vary the flavour of the marshmallows and biscuit crumbs to suit your taste – this is my favourite combination.

Time: 35 minutes

300g best-quality dark chocolate, chopped into small pieces
75g strawberry-flavour marshmallows, chopped into 1cm chunks
50g ginger biscuits, broken into small crumbs (not as fine as powder though)

Line a large baking tray with non-stick baking paper.

Melt the chocolate in a microwave, pulsing in 15-second blasts, and stirring in between until the chocolate is liquid.

Add the chopped marshmallows and stir to combine. Quickly – before the chocolate sets – pour it onto the baking tray and smooth out the mixture into a rough rectangle approximately 20 x 15cm. Immediately scatter over the pieces of biscuit and allow the chocolate to cool. When it is completely set, break it into rough pieces and store them in an airtight container or tin in a cool place.

Makes
300g

MARBLED CHOCOLATE BARS WITH CHILLI & GOLD

As Isabella writes in her Book of Household Management, *chocolate can be served at the end of the meal, presented with other sweet treats in decorative boxes. In fact, a small selection of homemade sweets served with coffee can replace a dessert course altogether if well chosen and presented attractively. This white and dark chocolate confection is easy, yet impressive.*

Time: 35 minutes

100g best-quality white
  chocolate, chopped into
  small pieces
200g best-quality dark
  chocolate, chopped into
  small pieces
Edible gold leaf (see
  Suppliers on page 202)
¼ tsp dried chilli flakes
  or to taste

You'll also need
Soft small clean paintbrush

Line a large baking tray with non-stick baking paper.

Melt the chocolates separately in a microwave, pulsing in 15-second blasts, and stirring in between until the chocolate is liquid. Using a teaspoon, blob the white chocolate onto the tray, spreading the blobs out a little with the tip of the spoon. Tap the tray lightly on your worktop to flatten the blobs. Make sure the dark chocolate is still quite liquid before you pour it on top, then pour it over the white chocolate and in between the blobs. You are aiming for a thin layer all over the white chocolate blobs. Tap the tray lightly as before, and use a small spoon to swirl the chocolates together, tapping the tray once or twice as you go to ensure that the chocolate layer is complete and there are no gaps. Sprinkle the chilli flakes over the surface while the chocolate is still warm, then allow it to cool slightly, but not set, before applying the gold leaf.

To apply the gold leaf, very carefully open the pack of leaf, and use a soft small paintbrush to pick up small pieces, placing them carefully onto the chocolate randomly.

Place the chocolate in the freezer or fridge until ready to serve. When you want to use the chocolate, break it into rough shards.

FONDANT, NOUGAT AND MARSHMALLOWS

Fondant, nougat and marshmallows are all based on simple sugar syrups cooked to different temperatures. The simplest fondant will be familiar to everyone as the basis of many filled mint and fruit chocolates and bars. Fondant shares many of the methods we use to prepare fudge, in that the hot syrup is worked until it forms fine sugar crystals and sets. It can then be flavoured and coloured to taste and dipped in melted chocolate if desired. The basic recipe for fondant on page 184 is a very useful starting point if you are new to these types of sweet as it forms the basis of all the other fondant recipes in this chapter.

Marshmallows and nougat, on the other hand, are more complex mixtures resembling cooked meringues with the addition of fruit, nuts and flavouring.

Fresh fruit juices feature in the recipes for marshmallows, which elevate these sweets way above those you can buy in the shops. Once you have mastered the art of making marshmallows, you can vary the flavours of juices you use, so long as you stick to the basic quantities given.

Nougat has its origins, like many of our confections, in the sweets of the Mediterranean and varies in its traditional form from the soft, chewy Montélimar types of France to the turrón of Spain that tends to be harder and more brittle, and which has links to Middle-Eastern sweets. In practical terms, the recipes are very similar, but to achieve the hardness required in turrón the syrup is cooked to a higher temperature, nearer to that of a caramel or boiled sweet so that the final result has a pleasing firmness.

The sweets in this chapter are some of the more complicated in the book, but all are easily achieved so long as you ensure that you have everything in place for the recipe before you begin.

TIPS AND TECHNIQUES

COOKING AND HANDLING HOT SYRUPS

For advice on cooking hot sugar syrups, please refer to the technical advice on pages 28 and 29.

FONDANT

Creamy in texture, pure white in colour, fondant is made from a simple sugar syrup that is cooked to a specific temperature, 116°C – about the same as fudge. The syrup is cooled by stirring on a marble slab, granite surface or in a large baking tray until it is firm enough to knead into a soft mass. When allowed to sit overnight, the fondant is said to 'ripen', meaning that the sugar crystals even out to a smooth, fine texture. Ripe fondant is creamy and not noticeably crystalline in texture. It can be flavoured and dried to make discs or logs which can be dipped in chocolate and decorated.

Flavouring and colouring fondant

Concentrated colour pastes are the best to use with fondant as they will not make the fondant more liquid. Go for natural flavour extracts rather than artificial essences. Floral flavourings are popular and traditional, with rose and violet creams being perhaps the most famous. Mint and lime also work well, especially with dark chocolate coatings.

Drying fondant

When fondant has been ripened, it can be rolled out and cut into shapes that need to dry and firm up before they can be dipped. In humid weather this can take a long time as the fondant tends to absorb moisture from the air. Do not be tempted to dry the fondant out in an oven – even the heat of a cool oven will melt the fondant.

Buying ready-made fondant

Good-quality ready-made fondant is widely available, but you should avoid ready-flavoured fondant if you want to add your own flavour to it.

NOUGAT

Super-sweet nougat recipes are based on syrups cooked to 143–149°C and mixed with beaten egg whites, often with added nuts, fruit and spice. Sweets similar to nougat are made across the Middle East, from Iran to Europe, where they are particularly popular in Spain, Italy and France. The degree to which the sugar is cooked to determines whether the final product is soft (143°C) or firmer to hard – (149°C). It is commonly made with honey which, due to its high fructose content (see page 15) will brown and burn at these temperatures, so recipes commonly cook two syrups, adding a honey syrup to the egg whites first before adding the higher temperature sugar syrup. Final additions of roasted nuts and dried fruits are added for interest and flavour; almonds and pistachios are popular choices. A free-standing food mixer is necessary to whisk the mixture.

Beating and rolling nougat

The nougat recipes in this chapter use a relatively small number of egg whites, but you will still require a large mixing bowl or food mixer to beat the whites once the hot syrup is added as they will increase in volume substantially before falling a little as they cool. When the mixture has been cooled and beaten to a stiff mix (70°C or so) it is stable enough to add nuts and fruit and to roll out into a flat sheet, to cool and be cut when fully cold.

Even when fully cold, nougat is sticky. It is advisable to buy edible wafer paper to cover the nougat in order to make it easier to handle when rolling and cutting with a lightly oiled knife.

Storing nougat

Nougat will absorb moisture from the atmosphere and so should be kept in an airtight tin or container. It is best eaten within a week or two of being made. You may find that the texture becomes slightly mousse-like with time as it absorbs moisture, but this is not harmful.

MARSHMALLOWS

Soft and yielding, marshmallows owe their origin to a gel intended to soothe sore throats made from the mucilaginous roots of the mallow plant, *Althaea officionalis*. Today, marshmallows are more commonly made purely from water or fruit juice syrup, egg whites and gelatine. The resulting mousse-like confection can also be used as a filling or frosting for cakes.

Beating and setting marshmallows

As with nougat, marshmallow recipes use hot syrup (in this case cooked to 128°C) that is then poured on to beaten egg whites to make a stable meringue, or mousse, which in the case of marshmallows, is further stabilised with gelatine.

It is advisable to beat the egg whites in a large bowl or food mixer to beat the whites once the hot syrup is added as they will increase in volume substantially before falling a little as they cool.

Gelatine is best bought in leaf form as it is virtually flavourless. It needs to be soaked in cold water before it is squeezed out and added to a hot mixture to melt it. In the case of marshmallows, the egg white and syrup mixture is hot enough to melt the gelatine provided it is added immediately after the syrup.

Flavouring and colouring marshmallows

Marshmallow is very versatile as a mixture and can be coloured and flavoured by using different juices. Because the initial syrup is only cooked to 128°C, real fruit juices can be used as their flavour will not be spoilt by high temperature cooking. Use juices that have clear, bright flavours like strawberry, pineapple or lemon and that will stand up to the sweetness of the mixture. Colouring, if desired, can be added at the same time as the gelatine. Paste colours work best as they provide a concentrated colour without diluting the mixture.

Makes
600g

BASIC FONDANT

This wonderfully flexible filling is the basis for all the fondant recipes in this chapter and it can also be flavoured to suit your personal taste.

Time: 1 hour plus overnight
 ripening

500g granulated sugar
125ml water
2 tbsp liquid glucose
¼ tsp cream of tartar
Sunflower oil, for greasing

You'll also need
Large metal baking tray, or
 a marble slab or granite
 worktop, scrupulously
 cleaned
Temperature probe or
 sugar thermometer

Fill your sink with an inch or two of cold water as you will need to cool the base of the pan.

Place the sugar, water and liquid glucose and cream of tartar in a medium saucepan, and stir over a low heat until the sugar has fully dissolved. Raise the heat to medium-high and boil the syrup until it reaches 116°C. Use a pastry brush dipped in hot water to wash down the insides of the pan and prevent any crystals forming.

When the syrup is up to temperature, dip the base of the pan in the water-filled sink for a couple of seconds to arrest the cooking process.

Pour the syrup onto your metal tray or clean worktop, and allow it to cool for a minute or two.

Grease a palette knife with a little sunflower oil and use to fold the edges of the syrup towards the centre and, as the syrup thickens, swap the palette knife for a wooden spoon or heatproof silicone spatula, which will enable you to stir the thickening syrup more easily. Keep stirring, then knead the syrup with your hands as it cools and turns white. The syrup will eventually become crumbly and opaque. Continue kneading the syrup until you can mould it into a smooth ball, then place into a shallow bowl or dish and cover with a lightly dampened cloth.

You now need to leave the fondant overnight to ripen – this means that the sugar crystals will even out to a smooth, fine texture. Don't be tempted to put the fondant in the fridge as it will absorb too much moisture and smells of other food. This will keep indefinitely in an airtight tin or container in a cool place.

Makes
60

VIOLET AND ROSE CREAMS

Flower extracts and essences were fashionable in Mrs Beeton's time, and today we can get very good extracts from online suppliers. Rose and violet flavours are enduringly popular.

Time: I hour plus I day
  drying time
⸺

200g Basic Fondant (see
  page 184)
Violet extract, to taste
Rose extract, to taste
Purple and pink food
  colouring, preferably paste
  (optional)
Icing sugar, for rolling
300g best-quality dark
  chocolate, chopped into
  small pieces
Crystallised violet and
  rose petals

You'll also need
Vinyl gloves
2–3cm round cutter
Chocolate dipping fork
  or other small fork with
  fine tines

Don your vinyl gloves. Halve the quantity of fondant and flavour half with violet extract and the other half with rose extract. Colour each portion appropriately with a tiny amount of purple or pink colouring, if using, and knead until well combined.

Lightly dust your worktop with icing sugar and roll the fondant out to a thickness of 3–4mm.

Using the cutter, cut out discs of the fondant and transfer these to a tray lined with non-stick baking paper. Continue rolling and cutting until you have used up all the fondant.

Allow the discs to dry at room temperature for a couple of hours, then turn the discs and leave uncovered until firm and dry enough to handle – depending on how humid the weather is, this can take a day or more.

When you can easily handle the discs, prepare your chocolate. Melt it in a heatproof bowl in a microwave, pulsing for 15 seconds, and stirring before pulsing again. Be careful not to overheat it (see page 148).

Working quickly, dip each of the discs in the melted chocolate using a dipping fork so that they are completely coated. Tap on the edge of the bowl to remove excess chocolate, then transfer to a tray lined with baking paper. As you work you may find the chocolate thickens as it cools, so you may need to re-warm the chocolate by briefly pulsing it in the microwave. When the chocolate is still soft, place a small piece of crystallised violet or rose on the top of each disc.

The actual amount of chocolate you use depends on how fluid it is when you dip. If you have any leftover, store it in a cool place until you need it.

Allow the chocolate discs to cool at room temperature before storing between layers of non-stick baking paper in an airtight tin or container.

Makes
40–50

FRESH STRAWBERRY FONDANTS

Ripe, seasonal strawberries should be used for this confection – make sure that the fruit is not only ripe, but dry and clean before dipping. The recipe uses a strawberry liqueur – crème de fraise – to flavour the fondant, but this is optional.

Time: 1 hour plus 30
 minutes setting time

250g Basic Fondant (see
 page 184)
1 tbsp crème de fraise
Pink food colouring,
 preferably paste (optional)
100g caster sugar
40–50 clean, dry
 strawberries with stalks

You'll also need
Temperature probe
40–50 tiny paper cases

Knead the fondant to soften it slightly, then place in a heatproof bowl. Pulse in a microwave in 10-second blasts, mashing the fondant with a fork in between each pulse to equalise the heat.

It is important not to heat the fondant above 40°C, so carefully measure the temperature of the fondant between each pulse using a temperature probe. It pays to be patient. When the fondant reaches the desired temperature, add the crème de fraise and a tiny amount of pink food colouring, if using. The fondant should at this stage be liquid. If it is not, add a little additional liqueur.

Have ready a tray with your paper cases laid out and a shallow bowl filled with caster sugar.

Dip each strawberry halfway into the fondant, shaking each berry gently to release any excess. Transfer the berry to the caster sugar so that it picks up a fine coating, then transfer the finished berry to a paper case. Continue until you have used up all of the berries and fondant. Eat within the same day.

Makes
60

WHITE CHOCOLATE GINGER FONDANTS

This recipe uses some of our oldest confections — crystallised ginger and fondant — with one of our most modern — white chocolate — to create a spectacular sweet.

Time: 1 hour plus 1 day
  drying time

75g crystallised ginger (see
  page 156 or use best-
  quality shop bought)
200g Basic Fondant (see
  page 184)
Icing sugar, for rolling
300g best-quality white
  chocolate, chopped into
  small pieces

You'll also need
Vinyl gloves
Chocolate dipping fork or
  other small fork with fine
  tines

Don your vinyl gloves. Chop 50g of the crystallised ginger very finely, add to the fondant and knead until it is evenly distributed.

Lightly dust your work surface with icing sugar and roll the fondant out to a thickness of 5–6mm.

Using a sharp knife, cut the fondant into bars 3–4cm long and 1cm wide and transfer these to a tray lined with non-stick baking paper. Continue rolling and cutting until you have used up all the fondant.

Allow the bars to dry for a couple of hours at room temperature, then turn the bars and leave uncovered until firm and dry enough to handle – depending on how humid the weather is, this can take a day or more.

When you can easily handle the bars, prepare your chocolate. Melt it in a heatproof bowl in a microwave, pulsing it for 15 seconds, and stirring before pulsing again. Be careful not to overheat it (see page 148 for notes on melting chocolate).

Working quickly, dip each of the bars in the melted chocolate using a dipping fork until completely coated. Tap on the edge of the bowl to remove excess chocolate, then transfer to a tray lined with baking paper. As you work you may find the chocolate thickens as it cools, so you may need to re-warm the chocolate by briefly pulsing it in the microwave.

While the chocolate is still soft, cut the remaining 25g crystallised ginger into tiny slivers and place a piece on top of each bar.

The actual amount of chocolate you use depends on how fluid it is when you dip. If you have any leftover, store it in a cool place until you need it.

Allow the chocolate dipped bars to cool at room temperature before storing between layers of baking paper in an airtight container or tin.

Makes 60

MINT CREAM SQUARES

Fresh mint can be easily used to flavour confections, as it is here when mixed with fondant and coated in dark chocolate. Choose a variety of mint that has a clear, strong flavour such as spearmint or Moroccan mint.

Time: 1 hour plus 1 day
   drying time

Handful fresh mint leaves,
   very finely chopped
200g Basic Fondant (see
   page 184)
½ tsp peppermint extract
Icing sugar, for rolling
300g best-quality dark
   chocolate, chopped into
   small pieces

You'll also need
Vinyl gloves
Chocolate dipping fork
   or other small fork with
   fine tines

Don your vinyl gloves. Place the fondant in a large bowl, add the mint purée and peppermint extract and knead until the colour and flavour are evenly distributed.

Lightly dust your work surface with icing sugar and roll the fondant out to a thickness of 5–6mm.

Using a sharp knife, cut the fondant into 4cm squares and transfer to a tray lined with non-stick baking paper. Continue rolling and cutting until you have used up all the fondant.

Allow the squares to dry for a couple of hours at room temperature, then turn them and leave uncovered until firm and dry enough to handle – depending on how humid the weather is, this can take a day or more.

When you can easily handle the squares, prepare your chocolate. Melt it in a heatproof bowl in a microwave, pulsing it for 15 seconds, and stirring before pulsing again. Be careful not to overheat it (see page 150 for notes on melting and tempering chocolate).

Working quickly, dip each of the squares in the melted chocolate using a dipping fork so that they are completely coated. Tap on the edge of the bowl to remove excess chocolate, then transfer to a tray lined with non-stick baking paper. As you work you may find the chocolate thickens as it cools, so you may need to re-warm the chocolate by briefly pulsing it in the microwave.

The actual amount of chocolate you use depends on how fluid it is when you dip. If you have any leftover, store it in a cool place until you need it.

Allow the chocolate dipped squares to cool at room temperature before storing between layers of baking paper in an airtight container or tin.

Makes
60

CHOCOLATE DIPPED LIME FONDANTS

Flavour your fondant with lime zest and a little lime oil to taste when making this recipe – the oil can be very strong, but the end result is fabulous.

Time: I hour plus I day
  drying time

Zest of 3 limes
Green food colouring,
  preferably paste (optional)
1½ tsp lime extract or oil
200g Basic Fondant (see
  page 184)
Icing sugar, for dusting and
  rolling
300g best-quality dark
  chocolate, chopped into
  small pieces

You'll also need
Vinyl gloves
2–3cm round cutter
Chocolate dipping fork
  or other small fork with
  fine tines

Don your vinyl gloves. Put the lime zest, a tiny amount of colouring, if using, and the lime extract or oil in a large bowl with the fondant and knead until well combined. Lightly dust your worktop with icing sugar and roll the fondant out to a thickness of 3–4mm.

Using the cutter, cut out discs of the fondant and transfer these to a tray lined with non-stick baking paper. Continue rolling and cutting until you have used up all the fondant.

Allow the discs to dry for a couple of hours at room temperature, then turn the discs and leave uncovered until firm and dry enough to handle – depending on how humid the weather is, this can take a day or more.

When you can easily handle the discs, prepare your chocolate. Melt it in a heatproof bowl in a microwave, pulsing it for 15 seconds, and stirring before pulsing again. Be careful not to overheat it (see page 150 for notes on melting and tempering chocolate).

Working quickly, dip each of the discs in the melted chocolate using a dipping fork so that they are completely coated. Tap on the edge of the bowl to remove excess chocolate, then transfer to a tray lined with non-stick baking paper. As you work you may find the chocolate thickens as it cools, so you may need to re-warm the chocolate by briefly pulsing it in the microwave.

The actual amount of chocolate you use depends on how fluid it is when you dip. If you have any leftover, store it in a cool place until you need it.

Allow the chocolate dipped fondants to cool at room temperature before storing between layers of non-stick baking paper in an airtight container or tin.

Makes
60

ALMOND NOUGAT

Nougat varies a good deal in texture depending on how high a temperature the sugar is boiled to. This almond nougat is tender to the bite, the crisp almonds providing a tasty crunch in contrast.

Time: 1 hour

250g blanched almonds
Two 20 x 30cm sheets
  edible wafer or rice paper
340g medium to strongly
  flavoured honey
160ml water
2 egg whites (about 60g)
550g granulated sugar
120g liquid glucose
250g dried sour cherries or
  cranberries
Sunflower or almond oil, for
  greasing

You'll also need
2 icing rulers or pieces of
  wood about 30cm long and
  1cm square
Temperature probe or sugar
  thermometer

Preheat the oven to 150°C/300°F/Gas mark 2. Place the almonds on a baking sheet and bake in the oven for 20 minutes until golden – break a nut in half to check that they are cooked through. Set aside and allow them to cool.

Meanwhile, place one sheet of wafer paper on a clean, odour-free chopping board and line up the icing rulers or pieces of wood alongside. Lightly grease these (but not the paper) with oil.

Now prepare your syrup. Place the honey and 50ml of the measured water in one pan on a low to medium heat until the mixture simmers. Monitor the temperature and let it cook until it reaches 125°C. As it cooks, have the egg whites ready in the bowl of a free-standing food mixer. Place the sugar, liquid glucose and remaining water in a medium pan and place on a low to medium heat until the mixture simmers and the sugar is all dissolved. Let the mixture simmer gently, brushing down the insides of the pan with a brush dipped in hot water to prevent any crystals.

Once the syrup reaches the required temperature, remove it from the heat and turn your mixer to high to start beating the egg whites. As soon as they reach soft peaks, pour the honey syrup down the side of the bowl and beat the mixture until it is firm and glossy, then turn your mixer to low while you finish the second syrup.

Raise the heat under the sugar syrup to high and monitor the temperature. When it reaches 148°C, remove it from the heat and add it to the mixer bowl, turning the speed to high as you do. You will notice that the mixture increases in volume rapidly before falling gradually as the mixture cools. Beat the mixture for a minute or two before turning the speed down to low and allow the mixture to cool. Check the temperature from time to time – and when it cools to 80°C, turn off the mixer and scrape the mixture from the whisk.

Working quickly now, add the almonds and berries and mix, then pile the nougat onto the wafer paper you prepared earlier. Place the second sheet of wafer paper on top and press or roll the nougat into a rough rectangle using the rulers or pieces of wood as a thickness guide. Take care as the nougat will be very hot.

Allow the mixture to cool for 2–3 hours before cutting it into lengths about 4cm wide. Wrap these in cling film and cut the nougat with a lightly oiled knife into small pieces only when ready to serve. Store in an airtight tin for up to a week.

Makes
80

PISTACHIO AND FENNEL NOUGAT

Fennel seeds perfume this soft nougat that is delicious when served, perhaps with pastis, as an after-dinner digestif.

Time: 1 hour

350g unsalted pistachio nuts
Two 20 x 30cm sheets
  edible wafer or rice paper
340g lightly flavoured honey
160ml water
2 egg whites (about 60g)
550g granulated sugar
120g liquid glucose
2 tsp fennel seeds
Sunflower or almond oil, for
  greasing

You'll also need
2 icing rulers or pieces of
  wood about 30cm long and
  1cm square
Temperature probe or sugar
  thermometer

Preheat the oven to 130°C/250°F/Gas mark ½.

Place the pistachios in a small saucepan and cover with water. Place on a high heat and bring to the boil. Remove from the heat and drain the nuts. Peel the pistachios, removing the purple skin, and lay them on a clean baking sheet. Dry the nuts in the oven for 30 minutes while you prepare the nougat mixture.

Place a sheet of wafer paper on a clean odour-free chopping board and line up the icing rulers or pieces of wood alongside. Lightly grease these (but not the paper) with sunflower or almond oil.

Place the honey and 50ml of the measured water in one pan on a low to medium heat until the mixture simmers. Monitor the temperature and let it cook until it reaches 125°C. As it cooks, have the egg whites ready in the bowl of a freestanding food mixer. Also at this time, place the sugar, liquid glucose and remaining water in a medium pan on a low to medium heat until the mixture simmers and the sugar is all dissolved. Let the mixture simmer gently, brushing down the insides of the pan with a pastry brush dipped in hot water to prevent any crystals forming.

Once the honey syrup reaches the required temperature, remove it from the heat and turn your mixer to high to beat the egg whites. As soon as they reach soft peaks, pour the honey syrup down the side of the bowl and beat the mixture until it is firm and glossy, then turn your mixer to low while you finish the second syrup.

Raise the heat under the sugar syrup to high and monitor the temperature. When it reaches 148°C, remove it from the heat and add it to the mixer bowl, turning the speed to high. You will notice that the mixture increases in volume rapidly before falling gradually as the mixture cools. Beat the mixture for 1–2 minutes before turning the speed down to low and allow the mixture to cool. Check the temperature from time to time – and when it cools to 80°C, turn off the mixer and scrape the mixture from the whisk.

Working quickly now, add the pistachios and fennel seeds and mix, then pour the mixture on to the prepared wafer paper. Place the second sheet of wafer paper on top and press or roll the nougat into a rough rectangle using the rulers as a thickness guide. Take care as the nougat will be very hot.

Allow the mixture to cool for 2–3 hours before cutting it into lengths about 4cm wide. Wrap in cling film and cut the nougat again with a lightly oiled knife only when ready to serve. Store in an airtight tin at cool room temperature for up to a week.

Makes 80

TROPICAL NOUGAT

Tropical fruits pepper this nougat with tasty, colourful nibs. Papaya, pineapple and mango all work well – sour mango would be even better if you can find it in healthfood shops.

Time: 1 hour

300g dried tropical fruit
 (pineapple, mango, papaya,
 mandarins)
Two 20 x 30cm sheets
 edible wafer or rice paper
340g lightly flavoured honey
160ml water
2 egg whites (about 60g)
550g granulated sugar
120g liquid glucose
100g flaked almonds
Sunflower or almond oil,
 for greasing

You'll also need
2 icing rulers or pieces of
 wood about 30cm long and
 1cm square
Temperature probe or sugar
 thermometer

Chop the pieces of tropical fruit to roughly the size of large currants.

Place one sheet of wafer paper on a clean odour-free chopping board and line up the icing rulers or pieces of wood alongside. Lightly grease these (but not the paper) with sunflower or almond oil.

Place the honey and 50ml of the measured water in one pan on a low to medium heat until the mixture simmers. Monitor the temperature and let it cook until it reaches 125°C. As it cooks, have the egg whites ready in the bowl of a free-standing food mixer. Also at this time, place the sugar, liquid glucose and remaining water in a medium pan on a low to medium heat until the mixture simmers and the sugar is all dissolved. Let the mixture simmer gently, brushing down the insides of the pan with a pastry brush dipped in hot water to prevent any crystals forming.

Once the honey syrup reaches the required temperature, remove it from the heat and turn your mixer to high to beat the egg whites. As soon as they reach soft peaks, pour the honey syrup down the side of the bowl and beat the mixture until it is firm and glossy, then turn your mixer to low while you finish the second syrup.

Raise the heat under the sugar syrup to high and monitor the temperature. When it reaches 148°C, remove it from the heat and add it to the mixer bowl, turning the speed to high as you do. You will notice that the mixture increases in volume rapidly before falling gradually as the mixture cools. Beat the mixture for a minute or two before turning the speed down to low and allow the mixture to cool. Check the temperature from time to time – and when it cools to 80°C, turn off the mixer and scrape the mixture from the whisk.

Working quickly now, add the fruit and nuts and mix, then pile the nougat onto the wafer paper you prepared earlier. Place the second sheet of wafer paper on top and press or roll the nougat into a rough rectangle using the rulers or pieces of wood as a thickness guide. Take care as the nougat will be very hot.

Allow the mixture to cool for 2–3 hours before cutting it into lengths about 4cm wide. Wrap in cling film and cut the nougat with a lightly oiled knife into small pieces when ready to serve. Store in a cool place in an airtight tin for up to a week.

Makes
60

LEMON AND MARIGOLD FLOWER MARSHMALLOWS

Edible flowers have been used for centuries to colour and flavour jellies and creams. Here, bright orange marigold petals are folded into the mixture to add spikes of colour to the finished confection. The English marigold (Calendula officinalis) is a cottage garden flower that is easy to grow. Omit them if unavailable, or substitute with dried lavender flowers.

Time: I hour plus 2 hours
   setting time

Juice and zest of 3 lemons
   (you will need 80ml juice)
150ml clear apple juice
400g granulated sugar
170g liquid glucose
200g egg whites – from 7–8
   medium eggs
Pinch cream of tartar
5 gelatine leaves
½ tsp citric acid
Yellow food colouring,
   preferably paste (optional)
2 tbsp English marigold
   flower petals (optional)
200g icing sugar
100g cornflour
Sunflower or almond oil,
   for greasing

You'll also need
Large baking tray – about
   20 x 30cm and 5cm deep
Temperature probe or sugar
   thermometer

Line the baking tray with cling film and lightly oil with sunflower or almond oil.

Place the lemon and apple juice, sugar and liquid glucose in a medium to large pan and stir over a low heat until the sugar dissolves.

Raise the heat and bring the mixture to the boil. Use a pastry brush dipped in hot water to wash down the insides of the pan to prevent crystals forming which would otherwise ruin your recipe.

While the sugar syrup boils, place the egg whites and cream of tartar in the bowl of an electric mixer and beat slowly. Place the gelatine leaves in a bowl of cold water to soften.

As the syrup approaches 125°C, increase the speed of the mixture until the mixture resembles soft peaks. Turn the mixer to low while the temperature of the syrup reaches 128°C. Then, increase the speed of the mixer again and pour the syrup down the inside of the bowl. When all the syrup has been added, squeeze any excess water from the gelatine and add to the mixture along with the citric acid and a tiny amount of food colouring, if using. Continue to beat the marshmallow until the mixture is very thick and glossy, then reduce the speed of the mixer to its slowest until the mixture is almost cold – this can take 10–15 minutes. Stir in the marigold petals, if using.

Pour the cooled mixture into the prepared tin and allow it to set for a couple of hours. When the mixture is completely cold and set, lift the marshmallow out of the tin and place it on a clean cutting board. Use a small sharp knife dipped in hot water to cut the marshmallow into 2–3cm squares, placing these on a tray lined with cling film.

Sift the icing sugar and cornflour into a bowl and mix well. Dust the marshmallows with this mixture to serve.

Store in an airtight container or tin at a cool room temperature for up to 3 days.

Makes
60

FRESH RASPBERRY MARSHMALLOWS

Dripped fresh raspberry juice lends a beautiful colour and flavour to these soft marshmallows. Our modern recipes are very different from their pounded mallow root ancestors, yet they are delicious.

Time: 1 hour plus overnight
   dripping time to make the
   raspberry juice and
   2 hours setting time

600g ripe raspberries
450g granulated sugar
170g liquid glucose
200g egg whites – from 7–8
   medium eggs
Pinch cream of tartar
5 gelatine leaves
Red food colouring,
   preferably paste (optional)
200g icing sugar, sifted
100g cornflour
Sunflower or almond oil,
   for greasing

You'll also need
Piece of muslin
Temperature probe or sugar
   thermometer
Large baking tray, about
   20 x 30cm and 5cm deep

To make the raspberry juice, crush the berries in a large bowl with 50g of the granulated sugar. Tip the mixture into a colander lined with muslin suspended over a large bowl. Cover and leave to drip in a cool room overnight. The next day, measure the juice. You should have at least 230ml. If not, make up the volume with clear apple juice or water.

Line the baking tray with cling film and lightly oil with a little sunflower or almond oil.

Place the raspberry juice, remaining sugar and liquid glucose in a medium to large pan and stir over a low heat until the sugar dissolves. Raise the heat and bring the mixture to the boil. Use a pastry brush dipped in hot water to wash down the insides of the pan to prevent crystals forming which would otherwise ruin your recipe.

While the sugar syrup boils, place the egg whites and cream of tartar in the bowl of an electric mixer and beat slowly. Place the gelatine leaves in a bowl of cold water to soften.

As the syrup approaches 125°C, increase the speed of the mixture until the mixture resembles soft peaks. Turn the mixer to low while the temperature of the syrup reaches 128°C. Then, increase the speed of the mixer again and pour the syrup down the inside of the bowl. When all the syrup has been added, squeeze any excess water from the gelatine and add these to the mixture along with a tiny amount of food colouring, if using. Continue to beat the marshmallow until the mixture is very thick and glossy, then reduce the speed of the mixer to its slowest until the mixture is almost cold – this can take 10–15 minutes.

Pour the cooled mixture into the prepared tin and allow it to set for a couple of hours. When the mixture is completely cold and set, lift the marshmallow out of the tin and place it on a clean cutting board. Use a small sharp knife dipped in hot water to cut the marshmallow into 2–3cm squares, placing these on a tray lined with cling film.

Sift the icing sugar and cornflour into a bowl and mix well. Dust the marshmallows with this mixture to serve. Store in an airtight tin in a cool place for up to 3 days.

PASSIONFRUIT AND PINEAPPLE MARSHMALLOWS

Makes 60

Sharp tropical juices work well in this recipe – balancing the sweetness of the meringue base. For added texture, chop about 150g dried pineapple or mango and scatter it over the surface of the marshmallows before the mixture sets.

Time: 1 hour plus 2 hours setting time

5 passionfruit
180ml pineapple juice
400g granulated sugar
170g liquid glucose
200g egg whites – from 7–8 medium eggs
Pinch cream of tartar
5 gelatine leaves
200g icing sugar
100g cornflour
½ tsp citric acid
Sunflower or almond oil, for greasing

You'll also need
Large baking tray – about 20 x 30cm and 5cm deep
Temperature probe or sugar thermometer

Line the baking tray with cling film and lightly oil with a little sunflower or almond oil.

Cut the passionfruit in half and spoon the seeds into a bowl. Add the pineapple juice, stir well and then pass the mixture through a sieve into another bowl. Measure the juice: you should have at least 230ml at least. If not, make up the volume with additional pineapple juice.

Place the fruit juice, sugar and liquid glucose in a medium to large pan and stir over a low heat until the sugar dissolves.

Raise the heat and bring the mixture to a boil. Use a pastry brush dipped in hot water to wash down the insides of the pan to prevent crystals forming which would otherwise ruin your recipe.

While the sugar syrup boils, place the egg whites and cream of tartar in the bowl of an electric mixer and beat slowly. Place the gelatine leaves in a bowl of cold water to soften.

As the syrup approaches 125°C, increase the speed of the mixture until the mixture resembles soft peaks. Turn the mixer to low while the temperature of the syrup reaches 128°C. Then, increase the speed of the mixer again and pour the syrup down the inside of the bowl. When all the syrup has been added, squeeze any excess water from the gelatine and add these to the mixture. Continue to beat the marshmallow until the mixture is very thick and glossy, then reduce the speed of the mixer to its slowest until the mixture is almost cold – this can take 10–15 minutes.

Pour the cooled mixture into the prepared tin and allow it to set for a couple of hours. When the mixture is completely cold and set, lift the marshmallow out of the tin and place it on a clean cutting board. Use a small sharp knife dipped in hot water to cut the marshmallow into 2–3cm squares, placing these on a tray lined with cling film.

Sift the icing sugar, cornflour and citric acid into a bowl and mix well. Dust the marshmallows with this mixture to serve. Store in an airtight container or tin at a cool room temperature for up to 3 days.

SUPPLIERS

Billingtons
www.billingtons.co.uk
Supply a range of natural unrefined cane sugars.

British Beekeepers Association
www.bbka.org.uk
For details of local beekeepers and honey producers.

The Chocolate Society
www.chocolate.co.uk
Supply the best quality chocolate from Valrhona and helpful advice on tempering.

Home Chocolate Factory
www.homechocolatefactory.com
Chocolate moulds, dipping forks, couverture and much more.

Lakeland
www.lakeland.co.uk
Nationwide and online kitchen shop that sells a large and excellent selection of kitchen equipment. Temperature probes, silicone moulds, dehydrators, airbrush kits and brilliant natural flavour extracts in large variety. Lakeland make a super spatula with a probe in it.

MSK Ingredients
www.msk-ingredients.com
Trade suppliers of specialist ingredients and equipment including crystallised flowers, fine nuts, fruit pastes and all kinds of flavourings and colourings. Also a good source of chocolate-making kit such as polycarbonate moulds.

Silver Spoon
www.silverspoon.co.uk
Silver Spoon produce all kinds of sugar from sugar beet grown in the UK and also supply pectin, golden syrup and treacle.

Squires Kitchen
www.squires-group.co.uk
A wide range of baking, chocolate- and sugar-work tools and ingredients, including silicone and polycarbonate moulds, lollipop sticks, couverture, edible wafer paper, food colourings and flavourings, silver and gold leaf.

Tate and Lyle
www.tateandlylesugars.co.uk
Offer various white and brown sugars as well as sachets of pectin.

Town and Country Fine Foods
www.tcfoods.co.uk
Supply excellent fruit purées in variety.

The Whisky Exchange
www.thewhiskyexchange.com
A wide range of alcohol for flavouring sweets including crème de violette and Marc de Champagne.

INDEX

Note: page numbers in *italic* indicate illustrations.

ACKNOWLEDGEMENTS

My grandparents, Harry and Elsie Hinch, allowed me free rein in their very traditional Yorkshire sweet shop where a marvellous variety of toffees, mints and jellies lined the shelves in large glass jars – thanks to them for their generosity and also to Eric Duodo, my dentist, for helping me get through my childhood with so little pain. Seasonal sweets always played a big part in our family gatherings – my mum's bonfire toffee in November, truffles at Christmas, and any time in between a range of fondants, marzipan and fruit jellies made regular appearances – so thanks to mum, Sandra, for her genius in the kitchen.

As always, thanks to Amanda Harris and Kate Wanwimolruk at Orion for their help and support during the genesis of this project and for putting their faith in me once again.

Matthew Canwell and Veronica Davidson at Lakeland deserve special thanks for their generous supply of flavours, colours and support through the weeks of recipe testing.

British Sugar and Tate & Lyle very kindly helped out with numerous queries and supplies of sugar – thanks to both.

Finally, thanks to Jenny Wheatley for providing the essential rigour that is necessary when editing such a large body of work, and to the creative team Loulou Clark and Julyan Bayes for their thoughtful and considered design layout.

First published in Great Britain in 2015 by
Weidenfeld & Nicolson, an imprint of Orion Publishing Group Ltd
Carmelite House, 50 Victoria Embankment, London EC4Y 0DZ
An Hachette UK company

1 3 5 7 9 10 8 6 4 2

A CIP catalogue record for this book is available from the British Library.

ISBN: 978-0-2978-7087-6

Photography by Kristy Noble
Art direction and props by Loulou Clark
Design by Us Now
Illustrations by Amy Borrell
Copy-edited by Jennifer Wheatley
Project edited by Kate Wanwimolruk
Proofread by Jane Sturrock
Index by Hilary Bird

Printed and bound in China

The Orion Publishing Group's policy is to use papers that are natural, renewable and recyclable products and made from wood grown in sustainable forests. The logging and manufacturing processes are expected to conform to the environmental regulations of the country of origin.

www.orionbooks.co.uk

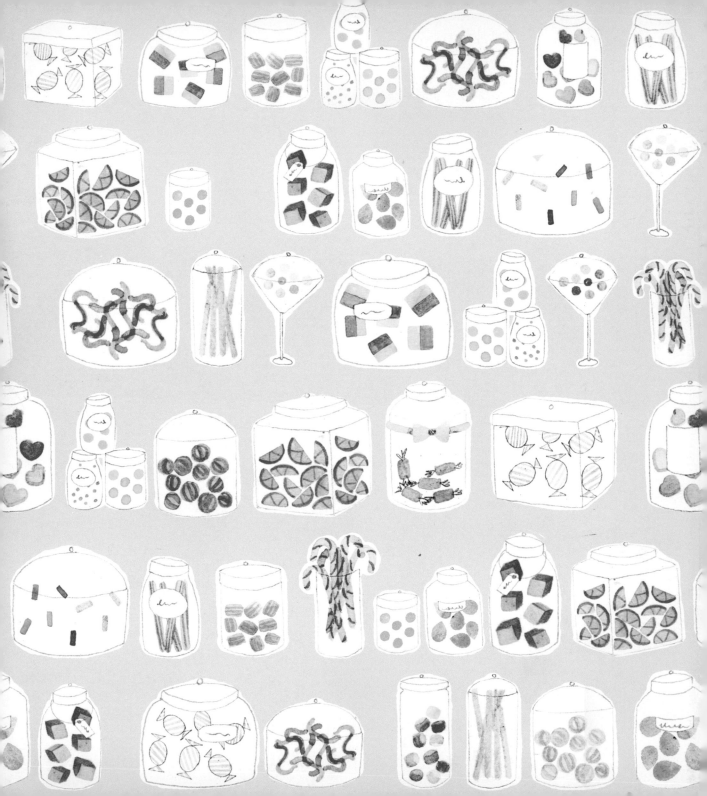